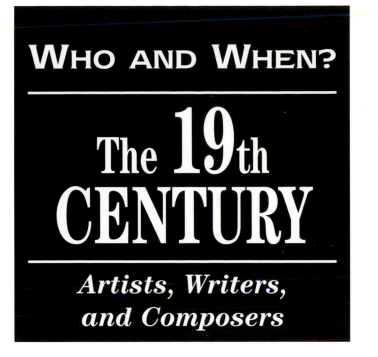

Who and When?

The 19th CENTURY

Artists, Writers, and Composers

WHO AND WHEN?

The 19th CENTURY

Artists, Writers, and Composers

Edited by Sarah Halliwell

RSVP

RAINTREE STECK-VAUGHN
P U B L I S H E R S
The Steck-Vaughn Company

Austin, Texas

Steck-Vaughn Company

First published 1998 by Raintree Steck-Vaughn Publishers,
an imprint of Steck-Vaughn Company.
Copyright © 1998 Marshall Cavendish Limited.

Library of Congress Cataloging-in-Publication Data
The 19th century: artists, writers, and composers / edited by Sarah Halliwell
p. cm. -- (Who and When? : v. 5)
Includes bibliographical references and index.
Summary: Introduces some of the major artists, writers, and composers that flourished
in the United States and abroad during the nineteenth century.
ISBN 0-8172-4728-9
1. Arts, Modern -- 19th century -- Juvenile literature. 2. Artists -- Biography -- Juvenile
literature. [1. Arts, Modern -- 19th century. 2. Artists. 3. Authors. 4. Composers.]
I. Halliwell, Sarah. II. Series.
NX454.A14 1998
700'.92'2--dc21   97-29888
[B]   CIP
                                                                                          AC

Printed and bound in Italy
1 2 3 4 5 6 7 8 9 0 LE 02 01 00 99 98 97

Marshall Cavendish Limited
Managing Editor: Ellen Dupont
Project Editor: Sarah Halliwell
Senior Editor: Andrew Brown
Senior Designer: Richard Newport
Designer: Richard Shiner
Picture administrator: Vimu Patel
Production: Craig Chubb
Index: Susan Bosanko

Raintree Steck-Vaughn
Publishing Director: Walter Kossmann
Project Manager: Joyce Spicer
Editor: Shirley Shalit

Consultants:
Anthea Peppin, National Gallery, London;
Dr. Andrew Hadfield, University of Wales;
Jonathan Kulp, University of Texas.

Contributors:
Iain Zaczek, Lorien Kite, Andrew Brown.

CONTENTS

INTRODUCTION

The 19th century was an age of enormous change. Improvements in technology transformed the way people lived. These developments offered new challenges to the arts, which were now appreciated by an ever-growing public.

The cause of much of the social change was the Industrial Revolution. Workers left the countryside and flocked to towns and cities in search of jobs. The wealth of urban centers brought new opportunities. Improvements in education meant that more people had knowledge of the arts, and extra money to spend on them. This meant, in turn, that the arts needed to appeal to a wider audience. While, at the start of the century, Jane Austen's tales of aristocratic life spoke to a narrow section of society, the novels of writers such as Leo Tolstoy (*see page 36*) were read by people of many different classes. The age range of readers was also widening, and the children's books of Lewis Carroll and Robert Louis Stevenson (*see pages 48 and 60*) appealed to an entirely new audience.

Artists and writers responded differently to the changes in society. Some, such as the Barbizon school of French painters in the 1840s and 1850s, turned their backs on the city, and instead produced images of the untouched countryside. But others, including the author Charles Dickens (*see page 24*) and Impressionist painters later in the century, found inspiration in modern urban life. Increasingly, too, artists and writers explored new subjects, such as psychology. The paintings of Edvard Munch (*see page 16*), and the plays of Henrik Ibsen and Anton Chekhov (*see pages 32 and 64*) all display a fascination with the human mind and soul.

The spread of industry brought disadvantages, however. The poor were often forced to live in crowded slums; many became involved in a bitter struggle for labor rights. Dickens used his writing to fight for improved housing and work conditions. As a result of the widespread hardship, the century witnessed a number of mass uprisings. These reached a peak in 1848, when most of Europe was caught up in civil unrest. Many disputes centered around nationalism. In central Europe, ethnic revolts threatened both the Austrian and Russian empires.

Nationalism also led to the creation of two new powers, Germany and Italy, both of which had previously been a collection of separate states. Richard Wagner and

Giuseppe Verdi (*see pages 80 and 76*) were closely linked to the independence movements in their homelands. The German composer had to live in exile after taking part in a rebellion, while Verdi's operas often contained political comments.

In the United States, too, the emphasis was on nation-building. During the course of the century, the American population soared from 5.3 million to 76 million, mostly through immigration. These new citizens helped to roll back the frontiers of their adopted home. In 1803, Ohio became the 17th state in the Union. In the same year, the entire Louisiana territory was purchased from the French: Part or all of 15 states eventually were carved out of this area. By 1821, six more states had joined the Union. Then, following victory in the Mexican-American War in 1848, the United States gained the present states of California, Nevada, and Utah, and parts of present-day Arizona, New Mexico, Colorado, and Wyoming.

Some Americans disapproved of this territorial expansion, but few could deny the rich variety of their land, which was celebrated by a wealth of writers and artists. George Caleb Bingham (*see page 12*) produced fine paintings of life in the West, while Thomas Cole (*see page 8*), the founder of the Hudson River School of artists, portrayed the majesty of the eastern landscape. Similarly, Jack London's tales described his adventures in the frozen Far North (*see page 72*), while Mark Twain (*see page 52*) wrote of the ways and customs of the Mississippi River area.

The chief threat to the young republic came from the issue of slavery. In the early 1800s, the Mason-Dixon line acted as an unofficial boundary between the free North and the slave-owning South. This system lasted until the Civil War (1861-65), which turned family against family. The works of Walt Whitman and Louisa May Alcott (*see pages 28 and 44*) described the horrors of the conflict.

In the arts, many Americans still looked across the Atlantic for inspiration, and it was common for writers—such as Edith Wharton (*see page 68*)—to pursue their careers in Europe. Gradually, though, toward the end of the century, this situation changed. The unique voice of Emily Dickinson (*see page 40*) influenced later writers, while John Philip Sousa and Scott Joplin (*see pages 84 and 88*) were among the first American composers to have an influence on European music.

THOMAS COLE

Thomas Cole was the first great American landscape artist. In the second quarter of the 19th century, he produced beautiful and dramatic scenes of nature that were laden with moral significance.

Thomas Cole was born on February 1, 1801, in Lancashire, northwest England, the son of a struggling woolen manufacturer. As the family's financial problems worsened, his parents decided to leave England and start a new life in the United States.

In the spring of 1818, the Cole family sailed from Liverpool to Philadelphia. While his parents moved west to settle in Steubenville, Ohio, the 17-year-old Cole remained in Philadelphia, working as an engraver. Eventually, the family asked their son to rejoin them and engrave wallpaper designs for the new family business. Cole did not have enough money for the stagecoach fare, so he crossed Pennsylvania on foot.

A NEW CAREER

The wallpaper business was not successful, however, so Cole had to look for other ways to assist his family. Around this time, he met a traveling portraitist named John Stein, who introduced him to the technique of oil painting. Under Stein's influence, Cole decided to become a portrait painter.

Over the next few years, Cole painted portraits and stage scenery, decorated ceramics, and made copies of famous paintings. When his family moved across the Ohio River to Pittsburgh, he spent some time with them there. The city was not yet industrialized, and Cole often went sketching in the surrounding fields and forests.

In 1823, Cole moved back to Philadelphia, where he studied the art collection in the Pennsylvania Academy of Fine Arts, one of the first art institutions in the United States. There he discovered the work of the American landscape painters Thomas Birch and Thomas Doughty. Fired with enthusiasm, Cole lost interest in portraiture and instead devoted himself to the art of landscape painting.

Thomas Cole, 1837, by Asher B. Durand **Durand painted this portrait of the 36-year-old Cole when his friend and colleague was at the height of his career.**

The Course of Empire: Savage State, c.1836, by Thomas Cole
This work, the first in the "Empire" series, shows humankind beginning its conquest of nature. Cole makes his feelings clear: On the left, where nature runs free, the sky is sunny; on the right, above a human settlement, storm clouds gather, a sign of impending doom.

In 1825, Cole moved again, this time to New York City. He exhibited several of his new landscapes in a store window, where they caught the eye of a merchant called George Washington Bruen. A patron of the American Academy of Fine Arts, Bruen gave Cole money to travel up the Hudson River and sketch the Catskill Mountains in upstate New York.

A MASTER OF LANDSCAPE

Returning with his sketches, Cole produced three landscape paintings, which he exhibited with an art dealer. The works came to the attention of John Trumbull, the president of the American Academy. He purchased one, and helped launch Cole on the career

that would eventually make him the most famous landscapist in America.

Cole's landscapes were dramatically different from those of his contemporaries Birch and Doughty. While they favored soothing, gentle views, Cole was attracted to the more dramatic and colorful side of nature: waterfalls, steep drops, and shadowy valleys. He depicted swirling storm clouds, with strong contrasts of light and dark. Cole was fascinated by nature's life cycles; they inspired him to paint landscape not simply as scenery, but as a symbol of the human condition.

Throughout his life, Cole was a deeply religious man. He gave a moral quality to his landscapes, which were meant to tell stories. His most famous work, *The Oxbow* (1836)—which shows a bend in the Connecticut River—symbolizes humankind's conquest of America, and the consequent shift from wilderness to civilization. For Cole, this progress was not entirely beneficial. He saw unspoiled nature as a source of creative inspiration and delight, and he lamented the rush to clear forests and reclaim land. *The Oxbow* thus has a sense of loss and foreboding.

THE COURSE OF EMPIRE

In 1829, Cole traveled to Europe for three years' intensive study. On his return to the United States, he began his most ambitious project, "The Course of Empire." This series of five pictures depicts the evolution of civilization. Showing a landscape being transformed by human development, it questions humanity's ability to control nature.

The first two paintings, *Savage State* and *Arcadian State*, represent wilderness being tamed by humankind. The third, *Consummation of Empire,* shows the scene covered by roads, bridges, and magnificent buildings.

The fourth painting, *Destruction,* represents the fall of the civilization, as crowds flee from an invading horde, who hack them to pieces and destroy the city. In the final scene, *Desolation,* humankind has disappeared altogether. Balance and harmony is restored: Nature has reclaimed the landscape, and transformed the traces of human settlement into vine-covered ruins.

The "Course of Empire" series was generally well received when Cole exhibited it in New York in 1836. Some critics, however, objected to its pessimistic mood. Although they admired Cole's talents, these critics preferred "real" views, without Cole's moralizing or his suspicion of human progress.

In 1836, Cole married and settled in Catskill, New York, with his wife. With his friend, Asher B. Durand, he took sketching trips, from which he produced some of his most impressive landscapes, such as *Schroon Mountain*.

In his last years, Cole became less involved with the art world, and more immersed in religious thought. He continued to work on series of moralizing pictures. One such project, "The Voyage of Life"—a depiction of personal religious growth—occupied much of the last decade of his life. It was not as financially successful as "The Course of Empire" had been, however.

Cole died in 1848. An outpouring of praise for the artist followed. Ironically, "The Voyage of Life" was a huge success when it went on show later that year. The landscapists of the next decade, such as Frederick Church and Albert Bierstadt, proclaimed Cole their spiritual father even as they themselves were developing a more optimistic style.

MAJOR WORKS

1832-36	"THE COURSE OF EMPIRE" SERIES
1836	THE OXBOW
1838	SCHROON MOUNTAIN
1839-48	"THE VOYAGE OF LIFE" SERIES

GEORGE CALEB BINGHAM

Bingham was the first major painter of the American West. His humble and serene scenes of everyday life helped shape the image of the United States western frontier during the nation's years of expansion.

George Caleb Bingham was born on March 20, 1811, in Virginia's Shenandoah Valley. His parents, Henry and Mary, owned a flour mill. As a boy, George drew constantly, anywhere and on anything, including the mill walls.

In 1818, the Binghams lost control of the mill, and moved west with their six children to the Missouri Territory. The family settled in the town of Franklin, on the Missouri River. There, Henry Bingham ran an inn catering to the river traffic. One of the visitors to the inn was the portraitist Chester Harding. While he was in Franklin, Harding painted a number of portraits. The nine-year-old Bingham worked as his assistant.

In 1823, Henry Bingham died of malaria, leaving his wife with a large family and sizable debts. Mary kept the family together by opening a school for girls. To teach art, she hired a woman named Mattie Wood, who became Bingham's first art teacher.

In 1825, tragedy struck again. The Missouri River flooded its banks and the entire town of Franklin was washed away. The homeless Bingham family moved across the river to a hamlet inhabited by fur trappers, traders, and boatmen—the people who would later become some of the most important subjects of Bingham's work.

AN ARTIST'S PROFESSION

At this stage, Bingham was still not certain that he wanted to become an artist. In fact, he started his working life apprenticed to a cabinetmaker, for a while thought about taking up law, and even briefly tried preaching. By 1831, however, he had decided to earn his living by painting portraits.

After getting married in 1836, Bingham traveled constantly to find work. His travels took him south to Mississippi, and east to New York and Philadelphia. In Philadelphia, he dis-

Self-portrait, 1849/50,
by George Caleb Bingham
Bingham painted himself shortly after he won a seat in the Missouri state legislature.

The Jolly Flatboatmen, 1846, by George Caleb Bingham
This picture of riverboatmen enjoying themselves after a hard day's work on the Missouri River is typical of Bingham's art. The painting became a national success when the American Art-Union bought it in 1846 and distributed engraved copies to its members.

covered the work of William Sidney Mount. He was America's leading painter of genre subjects—scenes of rural and everyday life. In genre painting, Bingham saw a way of representing the life and people he knew in the West. In the meantime, portraits still offered him a way to earn a living.

With all this travel, Bingham spent little time with his family. But he returned to Missouri in 1840 with a plan: The family would move to Washington, D.C. There, he hoped to find work painting portraits of politicians, as well as commissions for paintings to decorate

public buildings. In the event, work was scarce, but Bingham took advantage of being in Washington to immerse himself in politics. He was a passionate supporter of the Whig party, which later became the Republican party.

In 1841, Bingham's first child, Newton, died, and the artist became severely depressed. After repeated moves and several separations, the family returned in 1844 to Missouri, where they were to remain. Bingham now became obsessed with the life and politics of Missouri, which affected his most important artistic work.

In 1845, he sent his earliest surviving genre painting, and now his best-known work, *Fur Traders Descending the Missouri*, to the American Art-Union in New York. The union had recently been established to market and promote the work of American artists. This was a very important role, for in the 1840s, few galleries and collectors bought American paintings.

Through the Art-Union, Bingham found a receptive market for his western subjects. He produced mostly tranquil scenes of rivermen and pictures of American Indians. His images were nostalgic and charming rather than realistic, and had a great appeal for the largely East Coast audience of the Art-Union. In 1846, the union bought Bingham's *The Jolly Flatboatmen* for $290, had the picture engraved, and sent it to its 10,000 members.

A POLITICAL LIFE

Meanwhile, in 1846, Bingham's political convictions led him to run for a seat in the Missouri state legislature. He lost a very close election, but tried again two years later, this time winning by just 23 votes. His wife, Elizabeth, died in child-birth shortly afterward, and Bingham soon remarried. He left his two surviving children with his mother.

In the early 1850s, Bingham began a series of ambitious political pictures, such as *County Election*. He wanted to represent the democratic process at work on the frontier. Western critics liked Bingham's election pictures, but the response in the East was much less enthusiastic. To an eastern audience, it was one thing to see rustic westerners working in the river trade, but quite another to see them throwing themselves into the political process—traditionally the preserve of the East.

DECLINING CAREER

In 1852, the Art-Union collapsed. Bingham commissioned engravings of his works, paying for them himself, but he could not match the success of the previous decade. He traveled to Europe, held several important positions in state and city government—including state treasurer and police commissioner of Kansas City—and dabbled in various business and artistic ventures. Eventually, in 1877, he became professor of art at the University of Missouri. Two years later, he died in Kansas City in relative obscurity.

When the passion for regional art revived in the 1930s, Bingham's work was rediscovered, and exhibited in New York. It remains popular today, evidence of America's eternal nostalgia for the lost world of the frontier—a world that Bingham's images helped create.

MAJOR WORKS

1845	FUR TRADERS DESCENDING THE MISSOURI
1846	THE JOLLY FLATBOATMEN
1847	RAFTMEN PLAYING CARDS
1850	THE WOOD BOAT
1857	THE JOLLY FLATBOATMEN IN PORT

EDVARD MUNCH

A traumatic childhood scarred Munch for life, and ultimately led to his mental breakdown. From the depths of his torment, however, he produced paintings that have become some of the most powerful images of modern times.

Edvard Munch was born on December 12, 1863, in Løten, a small farming community in southern Norway. A year after his birth, the family moved to the capital, Christiania, later renamed Oslo. In 1868, Edvard's mother died of tuberculosis. The wasting disease also later killed his favorite sister, Sophie. These events affected the boy deeply, and the fear of death would trouble him for the rest of his life. He later wrote of his childhood: "Illness, madness, and death were the black angels that kept watch over my cradle and accompanied me all my life."

EARLY CAREER

When he left school, Munch decided to be an artist. From 1881 to 1883, he attended the State School of Art and Crafts in Christiania. There, he met a group of young, unconventional writers and painters. These artists took many of their ideas from Paris, which was then the cultural capital of Europe. In 1885, Munch made his first visit there.

In Paris, he saw works by Postimpressionists such as Vincent van Gogh and Paul Gauguin. Their art taught him that painting could be much more than the mere imitation of natural appearances.

Inspired by what he had seen, Munch returned home to paint *The Sick Child* (1886). In this, he moved away from depicting the natural world. He was more concerned with conveying the feelings of sickness, pain, and death. From now on, he would represent emotions and the workings of the mind, producing images that stemmed from his own tragic life and unstable mental state.

In 1889, Munch had his first one-man show. The success of the exhibit convinced the Norwegian government to award him a scholarship to study in Paris. During his three-year stay there, Munch came under the influence of the Symbolist painters. Like him, the Sym-

Self-portrait, 1886, by Edvard Munch
The intense and troubled Munch painted himself the same year he produced *The Sick Child*, "the breakthrough in my art."

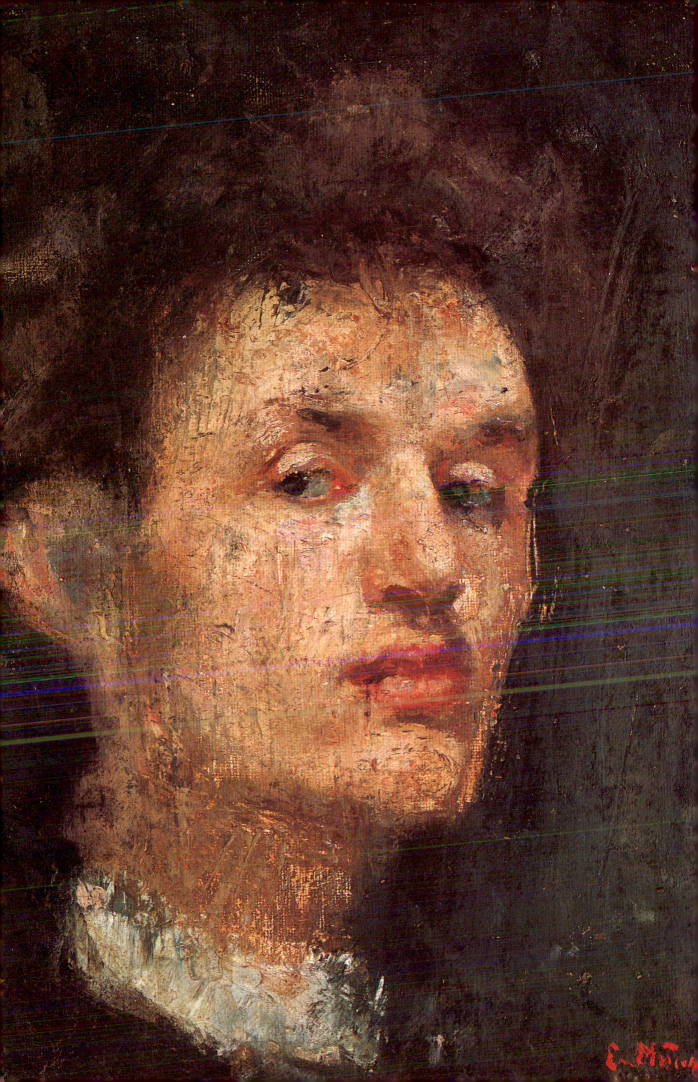

The Scream, 1893, by Edvard Munch

"One evening," wrote Munch, "I was walking along a path …. I felt tired and ill. The sun was setting and the clouds turning blood-red. I sensed a scream passing through Nature …. I painted this picture, painted the clouds as actual blood. The color shrieked."

bolists believed that they could express feelings, emotions, and ideas with paint.

In 1892, Munch exhibited his work in Berlin, Germany. His paintings caused such an uproar that the exhibit closed within a week. One critic declared that Munch's work "had absolutely nothing to do with art." The publicity made Munch so famous in Germany that he decided to move there. For the next 16 years, he lived in Berlin, traveling back to Norway for the summer months.

During this time, he worked on a series of paintings known as "The Frieze of Life." With titles such as *Jealousy*, *Hate*, and *Fear*, they expressed the passions, torments, and anguish that for Munch were at the heart of human existence. The series included some of Munch's greatest works, notably *The Scream*, a vision of panic that has become one of the most famous images of the modern world. It suggests the mind's terrible, irrational fears.

At the core of the "Frieze" series was Munch's view of female power. Women appear not only as powerful symbols of love, but also of death, capable of ensnaring and devouring their male "victims." These disturbing visions reflected the artist's own uneasy relations with women. His first affair, with the wife of a friend, haunted him for years, while another ended with Munch's girlfriend shooting off the tip of his finger.

BREAKDOWN AND CHANGE

In 1899, the Norwegian National Gallery began to buy Munch's paintings. Over the next few years, his reputation grew. He continued to lead an unsettled life, however, and was often short of money. His health also suffered from constant traveling. Things came to a head in 1908. After a three-day drinking spree, Munch suffered a severe mental breakdown. He was admitted to a Copenhagen clinic, where he stayed for the next eight months.

While he recovered, Munch resolved to change his life and his art. He gave up alcohol, and decided to stop traveling and to settle in Norway. He abandoned the obsessive, neurotic imagery of the past. He would now take his subjects from the world around him, rather than from the depths of the soul.

The breakdown marked the end of Munch's most creative period. Ironically, it also coincided with official recognition for the artist. In 1908, he was made a Knight of the Order of St. Olav, one of Norway's highest honors. And in 1910, he won a prestigious competition to decorate the assembly hall of Oslo University.

It took Munch six years to complete the project. The pictures show how radically his outlook had changed, for they are charged with an optimistic spirit and are painted in strong, fresh colors. These works, such as *The Sun* of 1909-10, represent positive, life-affirming forces.

Munch's final years were spent in isolation on his estate near Oslo. He lived a simple life, surrounded by his works, which he called his "children." Apart from a short break in the 1930s—the result of an eye problem—he continued to work until his death.

In 1940, during World War II, the Germans invaded Norway. Two years later, in December 1943, saboteurs destroyed a German ammunition dump near Munch's home. The blast blew out the windows of his house, and he caught a cold in the freezing weather. On January 23, 1944, he died of bronchitis: he was 80 years old.

MAJOR WORKS

1886	THE SICK CHILD
1893	PUBERTY; THE SCREAM
1894	FEAR; THREE STAGES OF WOMAN
1896-1902	VAMPIRE
1909-10	THE SUN

JANE AUSTEN

Jane Austen's six novels are among the most polished, controlled, and elegant social comedies ever written, full of sharp observations and wit. Yet her own life was quiet and modest.

Jane Austen was born on December 16, 1775, the sixth of eight children, in the English town of Steventon in Hampshire, a rural county southwest of London. Her father, Reverend George Austen, was a distinguished scholar, and her mother, Cassandra Leigh, was from an aristocratic background.

A GIRL'S LIFE

According to the custom of their class and time, Jane and her sister, Cassandra, lived very different lives from their brothers. While the boys received a classical education and went riding and hunting, the girls learned household management and "feminine" pursuits such as singing, dancing, and drawing.

In 1782, the Austen sisters were sent away to a school run by a relative, Mrs. Crawley. But after a short time, both girls became dangerously sick with fever. Jane was sent home to recover.

Jane's stay at home was short. She and her sister were sent away to school again in 1784. Back home after two years, they settled into a routine of helping their mother in the morning and receiving instruction from their father in the afternoon. Later, Austen was modest about her education. In fact, she had a thorough knowledge of English language and literature, could read French fluently, and knew some Italian.

Jane and Cassandra remained close as they grew up. They shared the same interests, and when they had finished their household duties, they enjoyed walking through the Hampshire countryside. They also frequently visited relatives and family friends. Jane spent much of her free time writing. Before she was 16, she had filled three notebooks with stories, poems, and plays.

As was usual in her social class, at the age of 16, Jane was launched into society and began to attend the parties given by families belonging to her own

Jane Austen, 1870, by Mr. Andrews after a sketch by Cassandra Austen
This delicate engraving was published 53 years after the writer's death.

genteel class who lived nearby. Guests enjoyed dancing at these local gatherings. There were also visits to the elegant spa town of Bath, in southwest England, where Austen experienced the aristocratic life that formed the background of her novels.

THE FIRST BOOKS

Throughout this period, Austen continued to write. By 1796, she had completed early versions of *Sense and Sensibility* and *Pride and Prejudice*. Austen's novels are about girls on the threshold of womanhood who are trying to find love and make good marriages. The subjects she chose were dictated by the fact that she was a woman. The opportunities open to her brothers—a good education, travel, financial independence—were denied her. Her literary skill lay in her ability to take something as simple as a few families living in a country village, and weave a story around their ambitions, hopes, and weaknesses.

A CHANGE OF SCENE

In 1801, however, the easy life in Steventon came to an end when her father retired and moved the family to Bath. They would spend five years there. The following year, a man seven years younger than Jane asked her to marry him. After accepting his offer, she changed her mind immediately and turned him down the next morning.

When their father died in January 1805, financial worries became constant for the family. Mrs. Austen and her daughters stayed in Bath another year

AUSTEN'S WORLD

Jane Austen based her fiction on the world she knew—the genteel, domestic world of women.

Jane Austen's world was tranquil and far removed from the traumas engulfing Europe at that time. Since her birth, the world had seen the American Revolution, the French Revolution, and the Napoleonic Wars. Yet she refers to none of these events in her novels. In her writing, Austen valued accuracy of detail and what she called "credibility" above all else. Therefore, she wrote only about things that she was familiar with, or that she had experienced. While dashing officers back home from battle regularly appear in her novels—described with accuracy and detail—Austen did not write

before moving to the port of Southampton, where they stayed for two years.

In 1809, Jane moved with her mother and sister to a cottage in Chawton provided by her brother Edward and close to Chawton Manor, his Hampshire estate. The move heralded the start of a period of great productivity for Jane and, for the remaining seven years of her life, her art blossomed.

about the fighting itself because it did not affect her directly. Similarly, nowhere does she portray men except in the company of women. And when anything upsets the order and calm of the lives of her female characters—elopements, duels, and death—it occurs offstage.

As a woman, her subject matter was limited to domestic life, social occasions such as glittering balls (*above*), and courtship. Yet Austen used humor and wit to express, in her own words, "the most thorough knowledge of human nature."

By now, Jane dressed in the style of an older woman, usually wearing a cap—then a symbol of middle age. She seemed to have abandoned hope of a social life, let alone marriage. The family had no carriage, so there was little chance to join in local life or make friends. Edward and his family were the only people nearby whom Jane could have met and talked to as an equal.

At Chawton, the Austens lived a quiet life. Jane prepared breakfast each day, and then practiced the piano. She wrote or read until lunch at midday. Afternoons were spent in the garden, walking, or shopping in the nearby town. The family often spent the evenings playing cards or games.

Her first book, *Sense and Sensibility*, written "by a lady"—since Austen wished to conceal her identity—was published in 1811, and it was well received. *Pride and Prejudice* followed in 1813, *Mansfield Park* in 1814, and *Emma* two years later.

FINAL YEARS

Writing took its toll on Austen's health. In 1816, she began to suffer from back pains and fits of fatigue. She was, in fact, suffering from the early stages of Addison's disease, which was then fatal. Her condition worsened, and she was told she did not have long to live. Early on July 18, 1817, her head on Cassandra's shoulder, Jane Austen died, aged 42. Two of her novels, *Northanger Abbey* and *Persuasion*, were published only after her death.

MAJOR WORKS

1811	SENSE AND SENSIBILITY
1813	PRIDE AND PREJUDICE
1814	MANSFIELD PARK
1816	EMMA
1818	NORTHANGER ABBEY; PERSUASION

CHARLES DICKENS

Charles Dickens was the greatest English novelist of his day. With bitter memories of his own childhood poverty, he devoted his writing career to campaigning against social injustice of every kind.

Charles Dickens was born on February 7, 1812, at Landport, near Portsmouth on the south coast of England. Two years later, the family moved eastward along the coast to Chatham, Kent, where Dickens's father, John, worked in the navy pay office.

In 1821, John Dickens lost his job and went to London with his family to look for work. He soon ran up large debts, and the whole family was thrown into debtors' prison. To help the family finances, the 11-year-old Charles went to work in a factory for a tiny wage. After about six months, however, a small inheritance cleared most of the family debts, and Dickens was able to leave his job and go to school. The trauma of imprisonment, poverty, and factory work would mark him forever.

By the age of 15, Dickens was working again, this time as a law clerk. The job was dull and undemanding, but it brought him enough money to enjoy London life, with its theaters, music halls, and taverns. Office life did not suit Dickens, however. Instead, he decided to become a journalist. At the age of 16, he got a job as a law court reporter.

THE ACE REPORTER

Before long, Dickens had become one of the leading journalists of his day, reporting the daily debates in the Houses of Parliament. He loved the work, but the experience gave him a lasting contempt for members of Parliament and for the establishment in general.

In 1833, Dickens, under the pen name "Boz," wrote a humorous short story for the *Monthly Magazine*. He received no payment, but was asked to contribute more of the "sketches." These caught the attention of a publisher, who asked Dickens to write a novel in 20 monthly parts. The result was *Pickwick Papers*, a series of comic tales describing the adventures of an

Charles Dickens, 1859,
by William Powell Frith
Dickens poses in his study for this portrait by the popular 19th-century English artist.

old gentleman, Samuel Pickwick, and his associates as they travel around England. The novel was hugely popular—at one point selling around 40,000 copies a week—and it brought Dickens fame and wealth. He now gave up journalism to concentrate on fiction.

In 1836, Dickens married Catherine Hogarth, and the couple moved into a new, large house in central London. At this time, he settled down to write his next work, *Oliver Twist*. In this novel, Dickens the social reformer began to overshadow Dickens the humorist. The book examined the plight of London's street children, who were corrupted by adults and turned into criminals.

A SOCIAL REFORMER

From now on, Dickens would use his fiction to fight all kinds of social injustice. Remembering his traumatic childhood, he attacked evils such as poorhouses, debtors' prisons, unscrupulous bankers, unjust courts, and cruel teachers who mistreated their pupils.

Dickens not only tried to bring about social reform with his novels but to entertain as well. He wrote with such imaginative drama and humor that he never seemed to be preaching a sermon. He was a master at describing a scene, whether it be a chase, a courtroom, a murder, or a dusty office. His characters are more virtuous, more villainous, more eccentric, more frightening, and more amusing than almost any other fictional creations. Uriah Heep, Betsey Trotwood, and Ebenezer Scrooge are just a few of the characters who seem to come alive in Dickens's books.

DICKENS'S LONDON

The bustling streets of 19th-century London were a constant source of inspiration for Dickens.

In Dickens's lifetime, London, with a population of three million, was the largest city in the world. Many of its citizens, however, lived in appalling slum conditions (*right*). In Covent Garden, at the heart of the city, 3,000 people lived in less than 100 houses. In one house, 37 men, women, and children occupied a single room.

This was an ideal breeding ground for disease. Typhus, cholera, and smallpox were all very common. The major cause of this was poor sanitation. Hundreds of sewers flowed into the Thames River, pumping filthy waste into the water. Even so, at low tide, children scavenged the river-

His fame spread, and in 1842 he toured the United States. When he landed in Boston, crowds gave him a rapturous reception. Everywhere he went, writers and politicians paid homage to him. In New York, 3,000 people attended a ball held in his honor.

In 1850, Dickens began editing the weekly magazine *Household Words*. He used the magazine to fight for social

banks for saleable items. At night, people searched the river for corpses, emptying their pockets of money and valuables.

Yet London also teemed with wonderful variety. Market traders, entertainers, beggars, gentlemen, and thiefs all rubbed shoulders in the lively, crowded streets. They provided plenty of inspiration for Dickens, who often roamed the city in search of material for his novels.

reform—campaigning for better housing conditions and sanitation, and for workers' rights—and to publish his own fiction, including his most savage attack on poverty, *Hard Times* (1854).

Household Words thrived for nine years, until Dickens argued with its publishers. He immediately launched a rival weekly called *All the Year Round*, which achieved an amazing circulation of 300,000. Like *Household Words*, it followed a formula of mixing fiction with articles on ideas and causes.

CRISIS AND SUCCESS

In 1856, Dickens bought Gad's Hill Place, a large house in Kent. By this time, his marriage was in crisis. Two years later, he and Catherine separated. Meanwhile, Dickens had undertaken a series of public readings of his work. They were a huge success. He was a gifted actor, moving listeners to tears by recounting the deaths of Paul in *Dombey and Son*, and Little Nell in *The Old Curiosity Shop*. Dickens went on many profitable reading tours in Britain and the United States.

But the constant traveling took its toll on his health. In the summer of 1870, Dickens returned home to work on *The Mystery of Edwin Drood*. After a few days, he collapsed with a stroke. He died on June 9, 1870. The news of his death caused worldwide sorrow.

MAJOR WORKS

1836	PICKWICK PAPERS
1838	OLIVER TWIST
1839	NICHOLAS NICKLEBY
1840	THE OLD CURIOSITY SHOP
1843	A CHRISTMAS CAROL
1850	DAVID COPPERFIELD
1854	HARD TIMES
1861	GREAT EXPECTATIONS

WALT WHITMAN

One of the most original and innovative of all American poets, Whitman was a passionate believer in human freedom. He wrote verse that celebrated the dignity of the individual and sang the praises of democracy.

Walter Whitman was born in West Hills, on Long Island, New York, on May 31, 1819, the second of six children. His father, a farmer-turned-carpenter, was mean and unjust. His mother, by contrast, was a kind and gentle woman to whom Whitman was always devoted.

In 1823, the family moved to Brooklyn, where Whitman attended school before dropping out at the age of 11. He then tried a number of jobs, including printer's assistant, printer, and handyman. After moving to Manhattan in 1841, he became a full-time journalist. Over the next few years, he worked on a number of newspapers in Manhattan and Brooklyn, including the *Brooklyn Daily Eagle*. At this time, he began writing short stories and a little poetry.

Whitman's job at the *Eagle* ended in 1848. He was fired for supporting the abolition of slavery. After leaving the paper, Whitman set off on an extensive trip across America. He was fascinated with the rivers, lakes, and hills, and with workers such as dockhands, laborers, and riverboatmen. These images of America would eventually find their way into his poetry.

After returning to New York, Whitman resumed work as a journalist. He was determined, however, to be a writer. In his notebook he constantly jotted down subjects to write about. Gradually, he turned away from prose, choosing poetry instead. He believed that the poet was more than simply someone who wrote verse. He saw the poet as a mystic visionary, a heroic figure whose role was to be the representative of the common man, freeing the human spirit through poetry.

LEAVES OF GRASS

In 1855, Whitman published a volume of 12 poems, *Leaves of Grass*. His poetic style in these works was simple

Walt Whitman
This photograph shows the poet in his fifties, a few years after experiencing first-hand the horrors of the Civil War.

yet full of detail. It was also highly original. Using coarse and frank slang, he wrote of subjects that at the time were considered vulgar and unworthy of fine poetry: the human body, common people's lives, and the noises and smells of the factory and the farm. He also ignored the traditional poetic conventions of rhyme and meter, preferring his own unique "free verse," which sounded like ordinary speech, but which some hostile critics condemned as disjointed and formless.

Although the book did not earn Whitman much money, many critics recognized the emergence of a bold new voice in poetry. While some attacked Whitman's indelicate subject matter and language, others acknowledged his genius. His innovations encouraged future poets to push the boundaries of verse even further. The originality and vitality of *Leaves of Grass* make it one of literature's most important collections of poems.

SILENCE AND RETURN

Over the next few years, Whitman wrote with immense energy. But in 1858, his poetry had to take a backseat to journalism, when he became editor-in-chief of the *Brooklyn Daily Times*. He continued to gather material for his poems, however. He often strolled for hours through the streets of Manhattan, or sat in restaurants observing other people eating their meals.

In 1859, Whitman began producing poems once again, but their mood had changed. They were now charged with a deep sense of death and loss. In these

THE U.S. CIVIL WAR

Divisions over the issue of slavery eventually led the United States into four years of bloody conflict.

In the mid-19th century, the issue of slavery divided the United States. While the North wanted to abolish the system altogether, the South was determined to defend it. During the 1850s, the dispute became increasingly violent, eventually leading to the outbreak of civil war in 1861 (*above right*). Over the next four years, until the North's victory in 1865, American fought American in a war that claimed more than 600,000 lives.

Although he did not serve in the Civil War as a frontline soldier, Walt Whitman witnessed first-hand the carnage created by the conflict. Upon the outbreak of

works, Whitman may have been expressing his fear of losing the ability to write poetry.

WASHINGTON YEARS

When the Civil War broke out in 1861, Whitman took a job as a nurse in a Washington military hospital. He continued to write, taking inspiration from his experiences in the hospital, where

fighting, he joined the North's war effort as a volunteer nurse in Washington, D.C. He visited the wounded, changed their bandages, wrote letters for them, and generally tried to comfort them in their agony.

Whitman's poetry contains moving imagery of his war experience. In "The Wound-Dresser," he wrote: "The neck of the cavalry-man with the bullet through and through I examine, / Hard the breathing rattles, quite glazed already the eye, yet life struggles hard, / Come sweet death! ...."

he was surrounded by suffering and death. He later published his war poems in a volume entitled *Drum-Taps*.

After the war, Whitman stayed in Washington, working for the government. His books now began to sell well, and he enjoyed a comfortable life. His poetry, however, began to change again. While his early poems were vividly concrete—the products of his observa-

tions and experiences—his later poetry was less detailed and more abstract.

As he got older, Whitman became increasingly concerned about the future of the United States. He feared that the country, full of poor people, was becoming like the corrupt countries of the Old World. In 1871, he wrote *Democratic Vistas*, the first complete survey of the United States after the Civil War. The essay was a scathing attack on American society, which Whitman believed was driven by greed and all kinds of corruption.

In 1873, Whitman suffered a stroke that left him partially paralyzed for the rest of his life. He now moved to Camden, New Jersey, where he stayed until his death. In his final years, he was widely admired as a bold, exuberant poet of the people, a champion for democracy and spokesman for the common man, although he often shocked people with his frankness. He grew a long, straggly beard, wore working-men's clothes, and publicly supported workers during labor disputes. He died in Camden on March 26, 1892, at age 72.

MAJOR WORKS

1855	LEAVES OF GRASS
1865	DRUM-TAPS
1871	DEMOCRATIC VISTAS; PASSAGE TO INDIA
1875	MEMORANDA DURING THE WAR
1891	GOOD-BYE, MY FANCY

HENRIK IBSEN

Always searching out new artistic challenges, the Norwegian playwright Ibsen created shock waves around the world with works such as *A Doll's House*, and sowed the seeds of modern drama.

Henrik Ibsen was born on March 20, 1828, in the timber port of Skien in Norway, about 100 miles southwest of the capital city of Christiania—now Oslo. He was the second son in a family of six children born to Knud and Marichen Ibsen. For the first few years of Henrik's life, his merchant father's business went well. But in 1834, Knud suffered a number of setbacks. In order to pay his debts, the family had to move to a small house at Venstop, two miles outside of Skien, where they remained for the next eight years.

AN EARLY CAREER

By 1843, Henrik had finished his schooling, and his parents decided that he should be apprenticed to an apothecary, or pharmacist. In December, he set off to begin his training in the town of Grimstad. It was a hard life: the hours were long, the work tedious, and there were few people around to talk to. Henrik began to read in earnest. He also started to write his first plays.

It was obvious that life as an apothecary would never suit him, so in 1850, Henrik set off for Christiania. In the capital, he became aware of the growing nationalist movement, which promoted the Norwegian language and folklore. Inspired by the nationalist mood, he wrote *The Burial Mound*, an epic historical drama about Vikings. He was delighted when the Christiania theater accepted it for production.

The National Theater in Bergen, a city in southwest Norway, offered Ibsen a contract as a writer in 1851. He remained there for the next six years. Yet he was dissatisfied, and in November 1857, he accepted a new post at the National Theater in Christiania.

The theater in Christiania had financial problems, however. In June 1862, it was declared bankrupt and Ibsen lost his job. For the next two years, he was to have no regular income. Ibsen and

Henrik Ibsen, 1895, by Erik Werenskiold
This calm and dignified portrait shows the playwright at the age of 67.

his new wife, Suzannah Thoresen, faced a tough future.

The 34-year-old began to travel. With a grant from the Norwegian parliament, he was able to spend 1864 and 1865 in Rome with his wife and son. Here, Ibsen produced his first great work. *Brand* (1866) is a verse drama about a preacher. The play was not staged for two more decades. In book form, however, *Brand* was an instant success.

Ibsen remained in Italy during 1866 and 1867 to work on his five-act verse drama, *Peer Gynt*. The story of Peer's slow journey to maturity on a number of fantastical voyages proved a great success with the Norwegian public. Ibsen was at last beginning to make a living from his writing.

A NEW DIRECTION

Ibsen now made two important decisions. He did not want to return to Norway. He preferred being away from his home country to write—even though his work was so essentially Norwegian. He would live and work in the German cities of Dresden and Munich until 1892. He also decided that he would no longer write in verse. He wanted to attempt something harder: to write dialogue in prose that actually sounded like real people speaking.

In 1879, Ibsen achieved his aims with *A Doll's House*. He pared back his cast to just five characters, confined them to a single room, and focused on a single theme: the lies and inequalities of marriage and their stifling consequences, particularly for women. The play was a startling success, and was rapidly trans-

A DOLL'S HOUSE

Ibsen's play of 1879 was an instant success—fueled by the scandalized reactions of audiences and critics.

A supporter of women's rights, Ibsen explored the subject in *A Doll's House*. The play tells the story of Nora, "the doll wife in the doll marriage in a doll's house."

When her husband, Torvald, is seriously ill, Nora secures a secret loan to take him to a warmer country. But she cannot repay the loan, and resorts to forgery. When her husband discovers this, he turns on her. Nora is on the verge of suicide, but realizes that she must move beyond the lies of her marriage, and find her own independence. Despite Torvald's pleas to rebuild their marriage, she leaves him and her children. As the play ends, Nora

lated and performed all over Europe. For the first time, Ibsen's fame spread outside his own country.

Nothing could prepare him for the shock wave of outrage that followed the publication of his next play, *Ghosts*, in 1881. As word spread about the play and its depiction of syphilis—a sexually transmitted disease—bookshops refused to stock the script and theaters

slams the door behind her, and steps out into a new life.

Ibsen's play questioned the sanctity of marriage and motherhood—institutions held dear in the 19th century. And it fired a debate about women's rights that still rages today. The play lives on, too: A production starring the English actress Janet McTeer in the role of Nora (*above*) was a huge hit when it appeared on Broadway in 1997.

would not produce it. In England, the play was banned altogether.

Ibsen was now notorious. His work took a new direction. The symbolism of *The Wild Duck* (1884) puzzled even his most loyal followers. His writing now reached beyond the realistic depiction of modern life. Ibsen now seemed to seek below the surface of life for more complex, hidden meanings.

With *Hedda Gabler* of 1890, Ibsen stunned his audience. He got rid of the speeches and explanations that an audience expected from a play. The characters in *Hedda Gabler* speak in single lines: It is the silences, and what is missing from what they say, that reveal the characters' inner lives. This discovery of "subtext"—a hidden meaning beneath the spoken text—was to have a huge influence on 20th-century drama.

In 1892, Ibsen wrote *The Master Builder*, believed to be his most autobiographical play. An architect's life is destroyed by the arrival of a young woman with whom he had once been infatuated. This story allowed Ibsen to explore many of his own fears.

In 1898, celebrations of Ibsen's 70th birthday began. But he was all too aware that his life was drawing to a close. In 1899, he wrote his most densely symbolic play, *When We Dead Awaken*. The following year, he suffered a stroke that left him unable to write. He survived for another six years, and finally died on May 23, 1906.

MAJOR WORKS

1866	BRAND
1867	PEER GYNT
1879	A DOLL'S HOUSE
1881	GHOSTS
1884	THE WILD DUCK
1890	HEDDA GABLER
1892	THE MASTER BUILDER

LEO TOLSTOY

Tolstoy wrote some of literature's most epic works, including *War and Peace*, which depicted life in 19th-century Russia with extraordinary skill. A wealthy aristocrat, he rejected his position and sought a simple life.

Leo Tolstoy was born on August 28, 1828, at Yasnaya Polyana—"Bright Meadow"—the family estate, 130 miles south of Moscow. At this time, Russia was still a feudal society, which meant that serfs, or peasants, farmed the lands of wealthy families like Tolstoy's. His parents were both dead by the time he was eight, and the family's five children were brought up by an aunt.

In 1844, Tolstoy went to a university, but left three years later without a degree. He read constantly, however—everything from the Bible to Dickens (*see page 24*). At this time, Tolstoy began his lifelong habit of writing journals. These are full of his beliefs and ideas.

BECOMING A LANDOWNER

In 1847, the Tolstoy estate was divided among the children. Leo received Yasnaya Polyana and the villages around it, which included some 4,000 acres and 330 peasants. He now divided his time between Moscow, where he had a lively social life, and home.

Tolstoy was restless, however. In 1851, he decided to go with his brother Nicholas to the mountainous Caucasus region to fight rebel Muslim groups. Tolstoy enjoyed both hunting and writing here. A fragment he had begun to write back home gradually grew into his first novel, *Childhood*. In July 1852, Tolstoy sent it to a magazine, *The Contemporary*, which published it the following year. It was an immediate success.

After leaving the Caucasus, Tolstoy took part in the Crimean War (1853-1856), when Russia fought the Ottoman Empire, Britain, and France. While stationed on the front, he wrote *Sebastopol Sketches*, battle tales that were published back in Russia. Tolstoy's sensitive stories of the soldiers and their sufferings boosted his reputation.

In 1855, Tolstoy returned to Russia. Although he became involved in literary

Leo Tolstoy, 1884,
by Nikolaj Nikolajewitsch
This portrait shows the 56-year-old writer hard at work.

life, making friends with other novelists, he was more interested in country life. Back at Yasnaya Polyana, he imitated the life of the serfs. He worked in the fields, believing that exhausting physical labor was vital for a contented life.

While Tolstoy felt he could learn from the peasants, he was determined to teach them, too. He realized that, if they were ever to be freed, the serfs would need to be able to read and write. So he opened a school at Yasnaya Polyana and taught the children himself.

When he was 35, Tolstoy met and proposed to Sofya Behrs, an 18-year-old doctor's daughter. He was not an easy man to live with. Before they got married, he made Sofya read all his diaries. This was the first of many challenges she was to face from her husband in the 48 years they were married.

WAR AND PEACE

The writer's settled family life inspired him to write in earnest. He began writing his masterpiece, *War and Peace*, in 1863. Sofya was unimpressed, writing in her diary: "He is writing of Countess So-and-So, who is talking to Princess Whosit. Insignificant."

War and Peace, published in 1869, is a panoramic portrait of Russian society from 1805 to 1812, including Napoleon's invasion of Russia. It is full of lively, colorful scenes—hunts, balls, and battles. It dwells on death and destruction, yet it has the effect of a joyful celebration of life. The novel made Tolstoy the toast of Russia.

Even in his early work, Tolstoy's skill as a writer is clear. He had an extra-

TOLSTOY'S RUSSIA

Tolstoy was born into a backward feudal society—in which serfs had few rights and no freedom.

Russia in the early 19th century was still a feudal society. This meant that a landowner—like Tolstoy himself—held power over his lands and his serfs. The serfs were essentially slaves, living in small houses on the estate, or in local villages (*above right*).

The landowners had once been soldiers. In 1480, Ivan the Great, dictator of all the Russian states, gave himself the title "czar," which means "Caesar." In order to create a loyal army, Ivan and other early czars gave land to professional soldiers, who in return served the state. These estates were then handed down from generation to generation.

ordinary ability to capture reality, highlighting all sorts of minute detail. He could bring a scene to life by using just a few sentences.

His next great novel, *Anna Karenina*, published in 1877, is a darker work. Anna is a beautiful society woman who is married to a government official whom she does not love. She falls in love with a society man, Count Vronsky,

By the time of Peter the Great, who ruled between 1682 and 1725, all nobles had to serve in the government or military for 25 years. The peasants, meanwhile, worked the soil.

Peter the Great tried to bring European reforms to backward Russia, but failed. Nearly 40 years later, during the reign of Catherine the Great, the aristocracy were finally freed of the obligation to serve the state. Controls over the serfs, however, were tightened. They were not formally freed until 1861, with the Emancipation Act

and leaves her husband. She tries to be happy in her new life with Vronsky, but is obsessively jealous of him. Desolate, she throws herself under a train.

A NEW PHASE
In 1879, Tolstoy suffered a spiritual crisis. He felt everything was hopeless, and death seemed to come ever closer. In the following years, he searched for new meaning and direction. At first he joined the Russian Orthodox Church, but left after two years. He also rejected the state, and challenged the all-powerful czarist government. He now devoted himself to political action and philosophical essays; his ideas would be highly influential all around the world.

It was not just his beliefs that changed. He also altered his lifestyle. Giving up his role as novelist and aristocrat, he now lived a simple life. He gave his property to Sofya, although he continued to live on the estate.

ESCAPING FROM LIFE
The publishing rights to his work then became the focus of a dispute between Sofya, who wanted the profits for the children, and Tolstoy's obsessive disciple Chertkov, who wanted power over his idol's reputation. Finally, Tolstoy could stand the "lie" of his life no more.

Before dawn on October 28, 1910, the 82-year-old stole away from home. He was heading for a monastery, where, as he wrote in a note to Sofya, he wanted "to live out my life in silence…." But he fell ill on a train, and was taken to the stationmaster's house at Astapovo, where he died of pneumonia.

MAJOR WORKS	
1853	CHILDHOOD
1855-56	SEBASTOPOL SKETCHES
1865-69	WAR AND PEACE
1875-77	ANNA KARENINA

EMILY DICKINSON

The mysterious poet Emily Dickinson wrote powerful and passionate works that reveal her obsession with death. She had just seven poems published during her lifetime; the rest were discovered after she died.

Emily Dickinson was born on December 10, 1830, in Amherst, Massachusetts, the daughter of a lawyer and his wife. The family was comfortably well-off.

Dickinson's older brother, Austin, and younger sister, Lavinia, would be her lifelong companions. Her parents were also alive for most of her own life; Edward Dickinson died in 1874, when she was 44, and her mother died only four years before Emily herself.

For a woman of her time, Dickinson was fairly well educated. Amherst was a college town. In 1840, she attended Amherst Academy, and seven years later moved on to Mount Holyoke Female Seminary.

In 1848, Emily, now 18, returned home without graduating. This may have been because her father wanted her to return home—or simply because she was homesick. She adored home, writing to Austin, who was away at Harvard: "Home is a holy thing—nothing of doubt can enter its blessed portals … here seems indeed to be a bit of Eden which not the sin of any can utterly destroy." From this time onward, except for a trip to Washington in 1855, and a few visits during the 1860s to a Boston eye specialist, Emily would never leave her father's home again.

RETREAT FROM SOCIETY

Slowly, she began to close herself off from society, and became known as the "Queen Recluse." She took to wearing only white, speaking to visitors from behind a screen, and creeping out by night to see the new neighborhood church, which her brother had designed. Austin had married Susan Gilbert in 1856, and moved into a house next door to the family's.

Yet this "retreat" did not happen all at once. Before 1860, Emily had friends at Amherst Academy, documented in letters. She was particularly close to a

Emily Dickinson
This undated picture of the writer probably shows her in her early thirties.

Manuscript of "Because I could not stop for Death," c.1863, by Emily Dickinson
This original manuscript, written in almost illegible handwriting, shows how Dickinson punctuated her work with lots of dashes and random capital letters.

clerk of her father's, Ben Newton. Some people think that it was his death, in 1853, that led to her seclusion.

Another reason for her willful isolation may have been Emily's frail health, combined with grief over the death of several friends and relatives. Some critics think that Dickinson's "retreat" was due to the breakdown of a particular love relationship.

Even after she withdrew from the world—"I do not cross my father's ground to any house or town"—Emily never stopped writing letters. They suggest that, far from being reserved,

when she liked a person she was obsessive. Her publisher, Thomas Higginson, commented, "Never have I met anyone who drained my nerve power so much. Without touching, she drew from me. I am glad I do not live near her."

Throughout her life, Dickinson enjoyed carrying on grand passions—but only from a distance, through the medium of deeply intense letters or poems. The more than 500 letters that exist are only a fraction of what she sent. She even wrote constantly to her sister-in-law, whom she adored—even though Susan only lived next door.

The bulk of Dickinson's work—1,775 poems—was not discovered until after her death. In Emily's bedroom, her sister Lavinia found the poems in "packets"—undated manuscript copies on folded sheets of stationery sewn together. None of them had dates or titles, and they were barely legible. But Lavinia decided that they should be published in memory of Emily.

DRASTIC EDITING

They were published in 1890, four years after the writer's death. But their impact was reduced by drastic editing. Dickinson had a strong taste for wildness and abandon in her poems, but early editors toned them down. They changed Emily's odd punctuation, which consisted of dashes and quirkily placed quotation marks and capitalizations. They altered words, and smoothed the poet's "gasping" style. They also added bland titles to the poems, although Dickinson never titled her work. These editors wanted to present her as a lady poet who wrote about "nature" and "mortality."

Still, Dickinson's work was so original that it bemused and surprised contemporaries. It tends to focus on death, using dark, intense imagery. Her famous poem, "Because I could not stop for Death – / He kindly stopped for me – / The Carriage held but just Ourselves – / And Immortality," is the chilling tale of her wedding union with Death.

Among the huge body of her work are some cheerful poems. One of the few works published in her lifetime, "Some keep the Sabbath going to Church" is written in the singsong rhythm and slightly lisping tone of a child.

Dickinson also had other interests. In 1856, she won second prize for rye bread at an agricultural fair, and the next year she judged the competition.

> "After great pain, a formal feeling comes – ... A quartz contentment, like a stone – ."
> (Emily Dickinson)

In July 1884, Dickinson had the first attack of her final illness described by a doctor as "revenge of the nerves." She died suddenly on May 15, 1886, possibly from a series of strokes or other neurological illness. She had known she was sick, but had not told anyone. It was not until 1955 that an edition of the poems using Dickinson's own punctuation and vocabulary was published.

MAJOR WORKS

1891-96	BECAUSE I COULD NOT STOP FOR DEATH; SOME KEEP THE SABBATH GOING TO CHURCH
1914	THE SINGLE HOUND
1945	BOLTS OF MELODY
1955	THE POEMS OF EMILY DICKINSON

LOUISA MAY ALCOTT

Louisa May Alcott dedicated herself to writing, and created one of the best-selling novels in the history of American literature, *Little Women*. Yet her family's demands on her meant that her life was anything but easy.

Louisa May Alcott was born in Germantown, Pennsylvania, on November 29, 1832. Her father, Amos Bronson Alcott, was one of America's earliest educational reformers. His strict teaching methods meant that he had few pupils and earned little money. His wife, Abba, found life very difficult. Not only did she have to cope with severe poverty, but also with bringing up four daughters—Anna, Louisa, Elizabeth, and May.

UNSETTLED EARLY YEARS

Louisa's parents criticized her constantly, telling her that she was too impulsive and opinionated. She grew up trying to be quiet and obedient—the way girls were expected to behave.

In 1840, when she was eight, the family moved to Concord, Massachusetts. Louisa was happy here, enjoying the countryside. But debts continued to plague the family, causing tension. From a very young age, Louisa helped her family with her earnings as a teacher, seamstress, and servant.

In 1848, Abba moved her family to Boston. Louisa felt trapped in the city after the freedom and beauty of the countryside, but she channeled her energy into staging plays for the family.

At the same time, she began to write. In 1854, at the age of 22, she published *Flower Fables*, a collection of short stories. She announced that she was going to be "rich and famous before I die."

Just as Alcott began to develop an interest in Boston's theater, the family moved to New Hampshire. Just five months later, however, Louisa returned to Boston to write and sell her stories. She lived with an aunt, sending money to her parents to pay off their debts.

In 1858, Alcott's sister, Elizabeth, died, and her elder sister, Anna, got married. Louisa felt left behind and betrayed. But political events would make these worries seem trivial.

Louisa May Alcott
The middle-aged Alcott takes a rare break from work to pose for this photograph. By this time, her writing had made her famous.

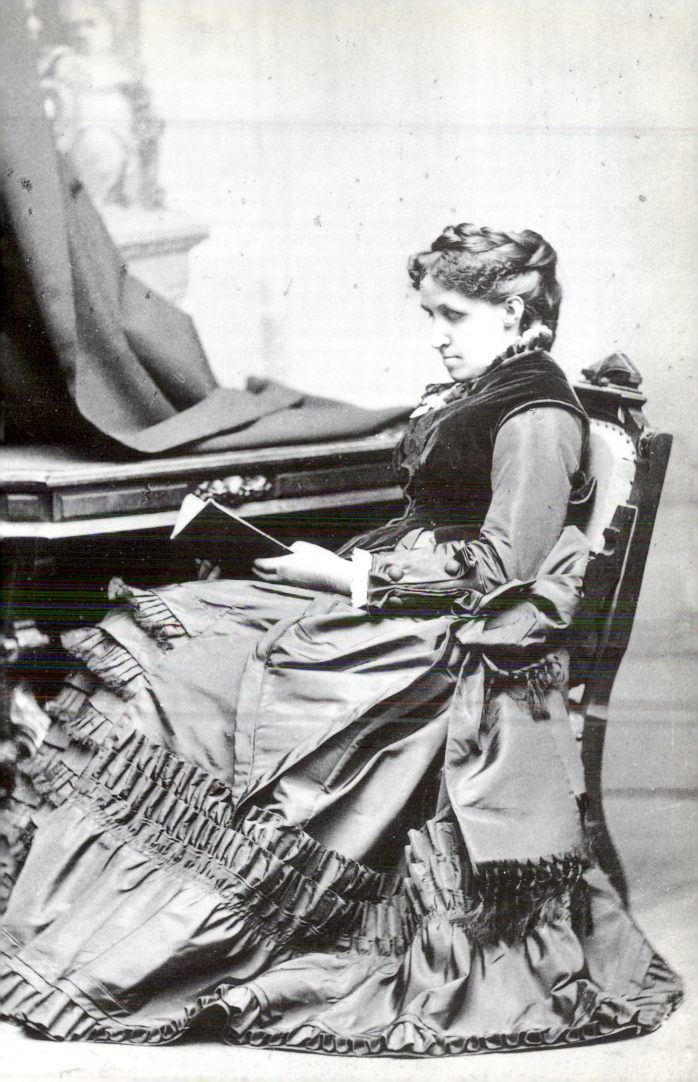

In 1861, the Civil War broke out. A year later, Alcott volunteered to be a nurse, and was assigned to the Union Hotel Hospital in Washington. She worked hard, but paid a price for her devotion, contracting typhoid. The illness affected her for the rest of her life.

SUCCESS AT LAST

Yet there were better times ahead. Alcott learned that *Pauline's Passion and Punishment*—a "blood and thunder" story, as she called it—had won $100 in a competition. In 1863, she earned $600 from similar gruesome stories. After 15 years of uncertainty, publishers were fighting for her work. Her dream of literary success was finally coming true.

In 1864, Alcott wrote *Moods*, in which she criticized the social restraints binding women. The following year, she traveled to Europe—something she had always wanted to do. But the journey left her exhausted, and back home, she collapsed. She spent the winter in her room, staying there for months.

After this black period came the high point of Alcott's career. In 1868, she wrote her masterpiece, *Little Women*. Both Alcott and her publisher doubted that the public would like the book: They were quickly proved wrong. The first year's royalties—author's earnings —of $8,500 enabled Louisa to pay off all the family debts. It sold a million copies in her lifetime, and remains a favorite for both children and adults to this day.

Readers loved the world of the *Little Women* and wanted more of the same. To meet the demand, Alcott produced a stream of novels, including *Little Men,*

LITTLE WOMEN

Louisa May Alcott's heartwarming tale, published in 1868, made her the idol of American girlhood.

Little Women tells the story of the March sisters, Meg, Jo, Beth, and Amy, who grow up with their mother while their father is away fighting the Civil War. The March girls' story is told in a series of episodes, each with its own moral point. Each sister has a different character and goal, and each has to overcome her own unique difficulties.

The central character, the tomboyish Jo (*right*), is based on Alcott herself at that age. Jo is wild and rebellious, driven by a fierce ambition to become a writer. Ultimately, Jo is tamed, fulfilling her father's wish for her to be a "little woman."

telling what happened to the characters when they grew up.

But despite her success, she did not enjoy her fame. She avoided the many readers who came to meet her. In her later years, although she had plenty of money, and her health was not good, she always felt a passionate urge to work. She poured out books, stories, and poems, as well as magazine articles

All the girls learn the virtue of self-denial. This was a virtue that all women were supposed to possess, and one that was vital to the 19th-century ideal of what being female meant.

Alcott describes the trials of growing up with tenderness and humor. The book is a warm-hearted celebration of family life and female virtues.

The strain of caring for Abba took its toll. Alcott became so ill that her elder sister Anna had to look after them both. When Abba died in 1877, Louisa was devastated, writing: "I shall be glad to follow her … a great warmth seems gone out of life." She would spend her final years looking after her father.

CARING TO THE END

In 1878, Alcott's sister May married and went to live in Paris. Two years later, May died after childbirth. Louisa adopted the baby, Lulu. But in 1882, when her father had a stroke, Alcott concentrated on caring for him, and Anna took over the care of Lulu.

Bronson lived for six more years. He was a demanding patient and Louisa's own health suffered. Against medical advice, she completed *Jo's Boys* in 1886. It was just as popular as the earlier books, and made her lots of money. Yet, even a year before her death, she still wanted to write: "Any paper, any pen, any place that is quiet, suits me."

On March 6, 1888, just two days after her father's death, Louisa May Alcott died. She was buried on Author's Hill in Concord, Massachusetts.

and advice columns. When writer's cramp paralyzed her right thumb, she learned to write with her left hand.

Now a celebrity, Alcott gave her support to the growing suffragette movement—the women's movement for equality. She traveled to meetings around the country. But she was torn between her interests and her duty to her sick and elderly mother.

MAJOR WORKS	
1854	FLOWER FABLES
1864	MOODS
1868	LITTLE WOMEN
1871	LITTLE MEN
1886	JO'S BOYS

LEWIS CARROLL

A shy, retiring man, Charles Dodgson only came alive in the company of children. Using the pen name of Lewis Carroll, he wrote *Alice's Adventures in Wonderland*—perhaps the most popular children's book ever written.

Charles Lutwidge Dodgson was born on January 27, 1832, the son of a clergyman. He spent an idyllic childhood in Croft, a small town in northern England. The eldest of 11 children, Charles wrote stories from an early age to entertain his younger brothers and sisters. He was a gifted child, having, in the words of his first headmaster, "a very uncommon share of genius." But he was shy, bad at sports, and had a bad stammer. As a result, he was constantly bullied. He was glad when he finished school in 1849.

In January 1851, Dodgson entered Christ Church College, Oxford, to study mathematics. What little confidence he had was shaken by the death of his beloved mother two days after he arrived, and he found it difficult to get along with the other students. Serious and hardworking, Dodgson got very high marks in his final-year exams.

Now 22, Dodgson remained at the university as a member of the faculty. He wrote many books on mathematics, but he was a terrible teacher. His students found him cold and unfriendly, with a complete lack of interest in their work. Dodgson's fame, however, rests on the writing and photography he did in his spare time.

AN INSPIRATION

He was inspired in both of these activities by a deep love of children. With small children, Dodgson lost his stammer and became witty and imaginative. He often carried with him a bag full of games with which to attract their interest, and loved entertaining them with his own stories.

The other great pleasure in Dodgson's life was photography. He was one of the great portrait photographers of the 19th century, pioneering a natural style that captured the spirit of his sitters. He took photographs of many famous people, but specialized in portraits of children.

Charles Lutwidge Dodgson
This undated photograph shows the writer in a typically reflective pose.

Scene from Alice's Adventures in Wonderland: *Alice at the Mad Hatter's tea party*
In Wonderland, Alice meets the March Hare, the dozy Dormouse, and the Mad Hatter, who all continually drink tea. They bewilder Alice with unanswerable riddles and nonsense.

Dodgson's gift for storytelling helped him in this, as he had to keep his young sitters still for hours at a time.

A GIRL CALLED ALICE

It was through his photography that Dodgson met Alice Liddell, the daughter of one of his colleagues at Christ Church. She enchanted Dodgson, and became the inspiration for the main character in the writer's first successful novel. Written as a Christmas present for his young friend, *Alice's Adventures in Wonderland* was published in 1856, under the pen name of Lewis Carroll.

The book begins with Alice sitting with her sister on a riverbank, bored and sleepy. Suddenly, a strange white rabbit runs by, muttering to itself. After following the rabbit down a hole, Alice finds herself in a strange land full of bizarre characters. In the course of her travels she meets the grinning Cheshire Cat, stops off at the Mad Hatter's Tea Party, and ends up as a witness at the trial of the Knave of Hearts, who is accused of stealing the Queen of Hearts' tarts. In *Alice's Adventures*, Lewis Carroll captures the atmosphere of a child's dream—which is exactly what Alice's adventures turn out to be.

Carroll's books differed from most of the children's books available at the time. These were often very dull, more concerned with teaching moral rules than providing entertainment. Carroll, on the other hand, encouraged children to behave and think like children. Alice is just a normal little girl trying to make sense of confusing surroundings. The land that she finds herself in is meant to remind children of the adult world, which often seems just as strange and illogical. Carroll believed that children can often see through nonsense that their elders take for granted.

A DOUBLE LIFE

Both *Alice's Adventures* and its sequel, *Through the Looking Glass and What Alice Found There*, published in 1871, sold extremely well, and gave Dodgson a regular income for the rest of his life. But Dodgson continued to work at the university, taking a lower-paid, but easier job at Christ Church—that of curator. This involved organizing the running of the college and supplying it with groceries, wine, and fuel.

Having a day job suited Dodgson, as he worked very slowly on his writing, piecing together ideas that he built up gradually over time. As a professional writer, he would have been obliged to finish work to deadlines rather than when he was satisfied with it. Dodgson declared that his books would have been "commonplace" and "very weary reading" had they been written under such circumstances.

Dodgson's double life sometimes caused confusion. Queen Victoria was so enchanted with *Alice in Wonderland* that she sent for the writer and asked him to send her a copy of his next book.

She must have been disappointed: The book she received was a complex work on mathematics by an Oxford professor named Charles Lutwidge Dodgson.

Although none of his other works achieved the popularity of the two *Alice* stories, *The Hunting of the Snark*, published in 1876, is regarded as one of the finest nonsense poems ever written. It began with just one line of poetry that came to Dodgson when he was walking. From the words "For the snark *was* a Boojum, you see," he created a fantastic adventure, full of strange creatures and invented words. Dodgson was bemused by the hidden meanings that scholars found in *The Hunting of the Snark*. "I'm very much afraid that I didn't mean anything but nonsense!" he claimed.

Success brought Dodgson many famous friends and acquaintances, but he never lost his shyness, except with young children. With *A Tangled Tale*, published in 1885, he used fiction to interest children in mathematics. In his later years, Dodgson suffered from ill health, and was often bedridden for weeks at a time. He died after an attack of bronchitis on January 14, 1898.

MAJOR WORKS

1865	ALICE'S ADVENTURES IN WONDERLAND
1871	THROUGH THE LOOKING GLASS AND WHAT ALICE FOUND THERE
1876	THE HUNTING OF THE SNARK
1885	A TANGLED TALE

MARK TWAIN

Adored for the warmth of his humor and his skill as a storyteller, Mark Twain wrote novels that captured the spirit of the South. Written in rich southern dialects, his works helped establish a literature that was truly American.

Samuel Langhorne Clemens, who became famous under the pen name Mark Twain, was born on November 30, 1835, in a village named Florida in Monroe County, Missouri. His father was a lawyer who had moved west to make his fortune in the frontier country. When Sam was four, the family moved to the town of Hannibal on the Mississippi. Sam grew up by the river, where he spent his time fishing, swimming, and watching steamboats pass.

In 1848, Sam became an apprentice printer at the *Hannibal Journal*, where his older brother, Orion, worked. At this time, he also began to write humorous sketches, one of which appeared in the Boston comic weekly *The Carpet-Bag*.

YEARS OF TRAVEL

In 1853, having learned his craft, Twain set off to work as a traveling printer. His travels took him all over the United States. In 1857, he met a famous riverboat pilot, Horace Bixby, and decided to become a river pilot himself. After an 18-month apprenticeship, he worked as a pilot for two years on the Mississippi.

In 1861, the Civil War broke out. At first, Twain sided with the South, but he soon switched his allegiance to the North. Finally, he gave up fighting, and went to join Orion in Nevada.

There was money to be made in this virgin frontier territory, but Twain was unlucky. His attempts at timber dealing and silver mining were unsuccessful. Writing proved a lifeline in these difficult days. He had several sketches published in the Virginia City *Territorial Enterprise*, and in 1862, he joined the newspaper as a reporter. It was while working on the *Enterprise* that he first used his pen name Mark Twain.

In 1864, he started another job, reporting for the *Morning Call* in San Francisco. He then tried his hand at mining for a second time, but again was

Mark Twain, 1935, by Frank Edwin Larson
In old age, Twain was easily recognized by his mane of white hair. Everywhere, people greeted him with rapturous applause.

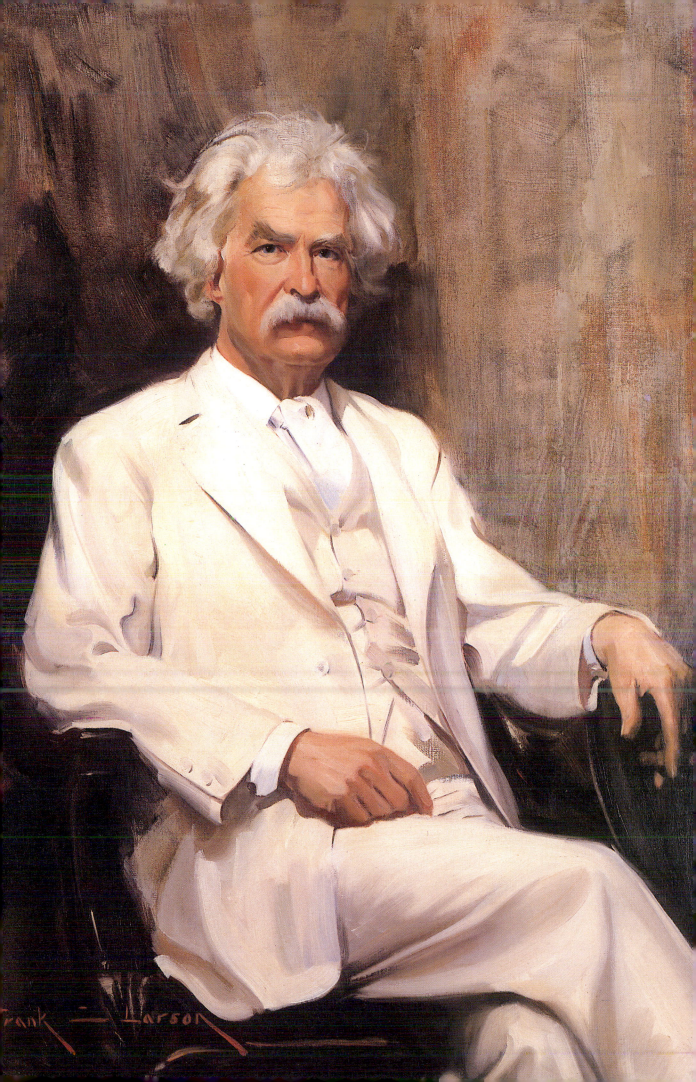

unsuccessful. One day, however, he heard a tale that caught his imagination. It was about a prize jumping frog. Twain wrote a story based on the tale, calling it "The Celebrated Jumping Frog of Calaveras County." The story appeared in the New York *Saturday Press* in November 1865, and in several other newspapers soon afterward. At the age of 30, Twain had become a writer.

Despite the story's success, 1866 marked a low point for Twain. He was short of money, was imprisoned for drunkenness, and at one stage contemplated suicide. But in March he went to Hawaii as a reporter for the Sacramento *Union*. His account of a sea disaster won him a reputation as a serious journalist. On his return, he set off on a highly successful speaking tour. He was an even more skillful performer with the spoken word than he was on the page. He often reduced his audiences to tears of laughter with his comic tales.

In 1867, Twain set off on a tour of the Mediterranean, recording his impressions in a series of letters published as *The Innocents Abroad* in 1869. With this book, he became the most widely read author in America. On the tour, Twain had become friendly with Charles Langdon, a rich young man from New York. In 1870, Twain married Charles's sister, Olivia. The following year, the couple moved to Hartford, Connecticut.

BOYHOOD TALES

In 1876, Twain produced *The Adventures of Tom Sawyer*, the story of a lively and adventurous lad from St. Petersburg, Missouri. He based the

HUCKLEBERRY FINN

Twain used his comic tale of a 13-year-old wanderer to comment on the southern way of life.

Most people consider *The Adventures of Huckleberry Finn* to be Twain's masterpiece. It follows the tale of Huck Finn (*right*), a friend of Twain's other well-known character, Tom Sawyer.

Huck's adventures begin when he escapes from his drunken and brutal father by faking his own death. He joins up with Jim, a runaway slave, and together they make their way down the Mississippi on a raft. All kinds of things happen to them on the journey. Huck witnesses a shoot-out between two feuding families; Huck and Jim meet two con men, who sell Jim back into slavery; and, finally,

book—a nostalgic, idealized picture of boyhood—on his own childhood experiences on the Mississippi River.

As soon as he finished *Tom Sawyer*, Twain began work on a sequel, *The Adventures of Huckleberry Finn*. This proved a much more difficult project, taking almost nine years to complete. When the book finally appeared in 1884, Twain was nervous about how the

Despite this criticism, *Huckleberry Finn* was a great success. Most readers loved its humor, its skillful use of American dialects, and its authentic re-creation of southern life, together with its important racial theme. Some critics now believe the book is the greatest American novel of all time.

MONEY PROBLEMS

In 1884, Twain had set up his own publishing firm. At first, he was successful, but by 1892 he was in financial trouble, having lost money through unwise investments. Two years later, he was bankrupt. He decided to go on a worldwide reading tour to pay back the $100,000 he owed. He set off in 1895. Everywhere, audiences flocked to hear him. By 1898, he was secure again.

In old age, Twain was a hero in the United States. As someone who had achieved fame and fortune from humble beginnings, he embodied the American dream. People loved him, and universities honored him. Even though he was suffering from heart trouble, and his health was poor, he continued to write until his death on April 21, 1910.

Tom Sawyer reappears to help Huck rescue Jim.

Besides being an adventure story and a comedy, *Huckleberry Finn* is also a moral tale. Huck ends up realizing that all human beings are equal—including slaves. In this way, Twain was expressing his own hatred of some of the values of the South, and especially of slavery.

critics would receive it. In *Tom Sawyer*, his central character had been a loveable young scamp, but Huck Finn was a mischievous 13-year-old thief, an enemy of respectable society. Twain had also written the story in the "crude" language of the Deep South, rather than "correct" English. One library banned the book because of this, saying it was "trash and suitable only for the slums."

MAJOR WORKS

1869	THE INNOCENTS ABROAD
1876	THE ADVENTURES OF TOM SAWYER
1882	THE PRINCE AND THE PAUPER
1884	THE ADVENTURES OF HUCKLEBERRY FINN

THOMAS HARDY

Hardy's novels shocked and outraged the 19th-century public for their bold treatment of human relationships and morals. Their honesty is still striking today. Yet he devoted the last 30 years of his life to poetry, his first love.

Thomas Hardy was born on June 2, 1840, in Higher Bockhampton, a small village in the county of Dorset in southern England. A delicate, sensitive boy, he spent his childhood in the family's isolated thatched cottage. His father was a stonemason who had a love of nature which his son inherited. Jemima, Hardy's mother, dominated his early years. Intelligent and lively, she adored Thomas, and had high hopes for him.

A GOOD EDUCATION

At the age of eight, Hardy went to the village school. A year later, he moved to another school in Dorchester, where he learned Latin, German, and French. At 16, he was apprenticed to John Hicks, a Dorchester architect.

Here, he met Horace Moule, who would remain Hardy's great friend for many years. Together they studied Greek, and Moule encouraged Hardy to write poetry. Six years later, Hardy moved to London, where a church architect took him on as an apprentice.

At this time, an article he wrote to amuse his colleagues, "How I Built Myself a House," was published. Hardy also began sending his poems to magazines, but none were accepted.

Hardy's first love was probably his cousin, Tryphena Sparks. She was independent, lively, and resembled Hardy's mother. Thomas and Tryphena spent a happy summer together in 1869, after which Tryphena supposedly gave birth to a son, although no birth certificate exists. The relationship did not last, however. Hardy found consolation in his poems and in writing his first novel, *Desperate Remedies*.

In 1870, Hardy went to Cornwall in the southwest of England to oversee the restoration of the church at St. Juliot. Here he met Emma Lavinia Gifford, the rector's sister-in-law, in a moment he later described as "magic." The

Thomas Hardy, 1893, by William Strang This portrait shows the uncompromising and moody writer at the age of 53, in a typically thoughtful mood.

Hardy's house

Hardy was born in this isolated thatched cottage, built by his grandfather in rural Dorset in 1800. He loved the beautiful countryside of western England where he grew up, and based his novels there, calling it a new name—"Wessex."

daughter of a rich lawyer, she had literary ambitions and energy.

In 1874, *Far From the Madding Crowd*, Hardy's tale of romance, betrayal, and tragedy in the English countryside, became a literary success. It was serialized in the popular *Cornhill Magazine*. Hardy was now fairly well off, and he married Emma. Ashamed of his humble background, he prevented his family from meeting her for two years.

A NEW LIFESTYLE

The couple settled in the countryside, and what Hardy called their "happiest time" followed. Both were excited by Hardy's newfound success, and Emma helped him by making notes for use in future novels. Their idyll did not last, however. Hardy's friend Moule had recently killed himself, darkening the

writer's view of fate for the rest of his life. In 1878, the Hardys moved to London, and Emma found herself left at home, bored and lonely, while her husband went to plays and parties.

Hardy wrote some of his greatest novels during this period—including *The Return of the Native* (1878), *The Mayor of Casterbridge* (1886), and *Tess of the D'Urbervilles*. The latter, published in 1891, tells the tragic story of Tess, an innocent country girl, who becomes a servant to a distant cousin, Alec D'Urberville. Alec seduces Tess, and she has a baby who dies. She later falls in love with Angel Clare, but he abandons her when she confesses that she has had a child.

The novel outraged Victorian moralists. Hardy subtitled the novel "A Pure Woman," and insisted on Tess's goodness throughout. This earned him a reputation for being immoral.

In 1895, Hardy wrote his most dark and controversial novel, *Jude the Obscure*. It centers on a stonemason,

---

"The ultimate aim of the poet should be to touch our hearts by showing us his own." (Thomas Hardy, 1879)

Jude Fawley, whose unconventional relationship with his cousin, Sue Bridehead, causes despair and tragedy.

Critics were shocked by the novel, calling it "Jude the Obscene." They particularly objected to its criticism of marriage as a "sordid contract based on material convenience." One bishop burned a copy in public. Yet the book sold an incredible 20,000 copies in the first three months of its publication.

Hardy's own marriage steadily deteriorated. *Jude* had outraged Emma, a religious woman. She felt that her husband was deliberately criticizing her own religious beliefs, and even tried to make him burn the proofs made of the book before publication.

On October 17, 1896, Hardy declared: "I have reached the end of prose." He was suffering from rheumatism, which made writing novels painful. He now devoted himself to his first love, poetry. Despite his worry that the public would reject them, *Wessex Poems*,

published in 1898, was an immediate success. During the last 30 years of his life, Hardy wrote more than 900 poems. It was as a poet that Hardy finally achieved the recognition he craved.

A SECOND MARRIAGE

In 1907, Hardy met Florence Dugdale, a Dorset woman from a similar background to his own. She became his secretary and, two years after Emma died in 1912, Florence and Hardy married. But Hardy then became consumed by guilt about his treatment of Emma, and wrote more than 100 tender love poems to his dead wife. The Hardys lived in a large, gloomy house called Max Gate in Dorchester, where Florence protected the writer from the outside world.

When Hardy died on January 11, 1928, his ashes were placed in London's Westminster Abbey, but his heart was buried in Stinsford Church, Dorset, with his first wife and parents. The humble native had returned to the country, hailed as a literary genius by the nation.

MAJOR WORKS

1874	FAR FROM THE MADDING CROWD
1878	RETURN OF THE NATIVE
1886	THE MAYOR OF CASTERBRIDGE
1891	TESS OF THE D'URBERVILLES
1895	JUDE THE OBSCURE
1898	WESSEX POEMS

ROBERT LOUIS STEVENSON

Robert Louis Stevenson spent most of his short life traveling the world in search of adventure. Through hard work and a natural gift for storytelling, he became the master of the adventure story.

Robert Louis Stevenson was born in Edinburgh, the capital of Scotland, on November 13, 1850. Like his mother, Margaret, Robert suffered from almost constant illness. He spent much of his childhood in the care of his nurse, or alone, dreaming of travel and adventure. His father, Thomas, was a wealthy engineer and inventor. A stern man, Thomas hoped that his only child would also become an engineer.

AN AMBITION TO WRITE

When he was 17, Stevenson went to Edinburgh University to study engineering. He was an idle student. His real ambition was to become a writer, and in 1871, he summoned up the nerve to tell his father. Thomas took the news calmly, believing that it was merely a youthful phase. He told his son that he must study law first, so that he would at least have a career should his writing fail.

During his student years, Stevenson rebelled against his strict, religious upbringing. He wore bizarre clothes, and spent his evenings in the company of Edinburgh's criminal low life. These people would later provide the inspiration for many of his fictional rogues.

In 1873, Stevenson met Sidney Colvin, a well-known scholar of art and literature. They began a lifelong friendship. Colvin introduced Stevenson to the London literary scene, and helped him to get work writing for magazines. Meanwhile, the young man passed his law exams. But he would never work as a lawyer; his heart was elsewhere.

For the next few years, Stevenson traveled around England, Scotland, and France, writing jokingly to his mother that he was "a tramp and a vagabond." Stevenson longed to escape from the cold, damp weather of his homeland, which did not suit him. He claimed that Edinburgh had "one of the vilest climates under the heaven."

Robert Louis Stevenson, 1887, by Sir William Blake Richmond
This painting shows the writer just before he left Britain for the last time.

In July 1876, at an artists' colony near Paris, Stevenson met Fanny Van de Grift Osbourne—an American woman with whom he would spend the rest of his life. Although she was ten years older than he, and had two children to support, it was love at first sight. He was devastated when she returned to America in 1878, but he set sail immediately when she invited him to join her a year later. They were married in San Francisco on May 19, 1880, and spent their honeymoon in an old silver mining shack—an experience the writer recaptured in *The Silverado Squatters*.

THE HEIGHT OF SUCCESS

After the honeymoon, Stevenson and Fanny, together with Fanny's son, Lloyd, sailed for Scotland. During their two years there, Stevenson wrote *Treasure Island*—his first and most famous novel. After a spell in the south of France, the family settled in the south of England, where Stevenson wrote three more classics—*A Child's Garden of Verses*, *Kidnapped*, and *The Strange Case of Dr. Jekyll and Mr. Hyde*.

Even at the height of his success, Stevenson lacked confidence in his own abilities. Writing did not come easily to him, and he often became very frustrated by his slow progress. "What genius I had was for hard work," he later told his stepson. He clearly did have a great talent for applying himself, however: He managed to write 20 books in the last 16 years of his life.

Although Stevenson was a wonderful storyteller, his books are more than simple adventure stories. His characters

TREASURE ISLAND

Stevenson's classic tale of pirates and hidden treasure has entertained generations of readers.

Treasure Island all began with a map Stevenson drew to amuse his stepson, Lloyd. "As I pored over my map," he wrote, "the future characters of the book began to appear there visibly among imaginary woods." Inspired, Stevenson wrote his first novel at breakneck speed.

The hero of Stevenson's tale is Jim Hawkins, a teenage boy. His adventures begin when an old sea captain comes to stay at his family's inn. The captain has a precious secret—a map showing where to find some pirate treasure . When the old captain dies mysteriously, Jim searches for, and finds, the map.

are complex, and are usually impossible to classify as wholly good or evil. This makes the action in his novels all the more exciting, as the characters involved are both believable and appealing. In *Treasure Island*, for example, the reader cannot help liking the colorful pirate Long John Silver for his cleverness and charm, even though he is a murderous villain.

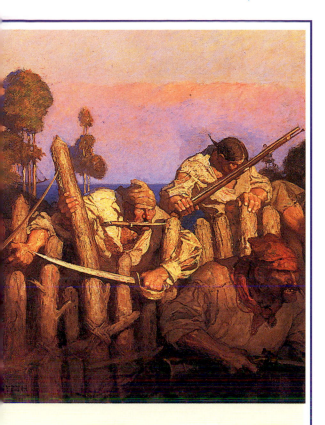

Jim sets off on a mission to find Treasure Island. Little does he know that most of his ship's crew are pirates (above) who want the treasure for themselves. Upon reaching the island, the pirates mutiny at the command of their leader, Long John Silver. This sets the scene for an epic tale of adventure.

After the death of his father in 1887, Stevenson, his mother, Fanny, and Lloyd went to America. The family settled for a year in the Adirondack Mountains, until Stevenson decided to turn a long-cherished dream into reality. It was to be his last great adventure.

Stevenson hired a boat—the *Casco*—and in June 1888, the whole family set sail from San Francisco Bay for the South Seas. The *Casco* took them to the Marquesas Islands, Tahiti, and Honolulu. The islands were even more wonderful than Stevenson had hoped. He wrote that he had gained "more fun and pleasure of my life these past months than ever before, and more health than at any time in ten long years."

A FINAL HOME

Stevenson found his final home in December 1889, at Apia, the capital of Upolu in the Samoan Islands. Here he built a magnificent wooden house, and settled there with his family. Stevenson was popular on the island, and became known to his Samoan friends as "*Tusitala*"—"teller of stories."

The writer was now 44, and feeling healthier than ever. Then, suddenly, on December 3, 1894, he died of a brain hemorrhage. He left an unfinished novel, *The Weir of Hermiston*. This book, set in 18th-century Scotland, contains some of Stevenson's finest writing, and many people think that it would have been his greatest novel had he finished it. He was buried at the top of Samoa's Mount Vaea.

MAJOR WORKS	
1883	THE SILVERADO SQUATTERS; TREASURE ISLAND
1885	A CHILD'S GARDEN OF VERSES
1886	KIDNAPPED; THE STRANGE CASE OF DR. JEKYLL AND MR. HYDE

ANTON CHEKHOV

In his brief lifetime, Anton Chekhov became the master of the short story, and produced some of the finest plays ever written. He was a compassionate man, committed to truth and justice in life as well as in art.

Anton Pavlovich Chekhov was born on January 17, 1860, in Taganrog, a small seaport in southern Russia. His father was a shopkeeper who struggled to provide for his large family. Chekhov was later to look back on his childhood as a miserable time, full of beatings and dreary church services. He attended the local school from the age of eight, but was unable to devote himself fully to his studies as he had to spend most of his time working in his father's store.

A STUDENT WRITER

In 1876, the store closed down. The family moved to Moscow, leaving Anton behind in Taganrog. The 16-year-old stayed in school, supporting himself by tutoring in his spare time. He moved to Moscow in 1879, and enrolled at the university as a medical student. His family were now desperately poor. To support them, Chekhov began writing comic stories for magazines.

Success came immediately. Despite the fact that much of his early work was rushed and careless, Chekhov published nearly everything he wrote. He had a fine comic touch, and the constant pressure to produce work for the magazines gradually ripened his talent.

COMMITTING TO WRITING

In 1884, Chekhov left the university. When his letters were published in the 1970s, it was discovered that he had left without completing his studies. Even so, he was still allowed to become a doctor, and for a while he ran a medical practice. But he continued to rely on writing for the bulk of his earnings.

After the success of his second book, *Motley Stories*, in 1886, he gave up his practice—although he was always prepared to treat needy cases. He was asked to write for a daily newspaper, *The New Times*, which meant higher rates and more prestige.

Anton Chekhov, 1897
This photograph shows Chekhov resting in his country home, around the time he discovered he was suffering from tuberculosis.

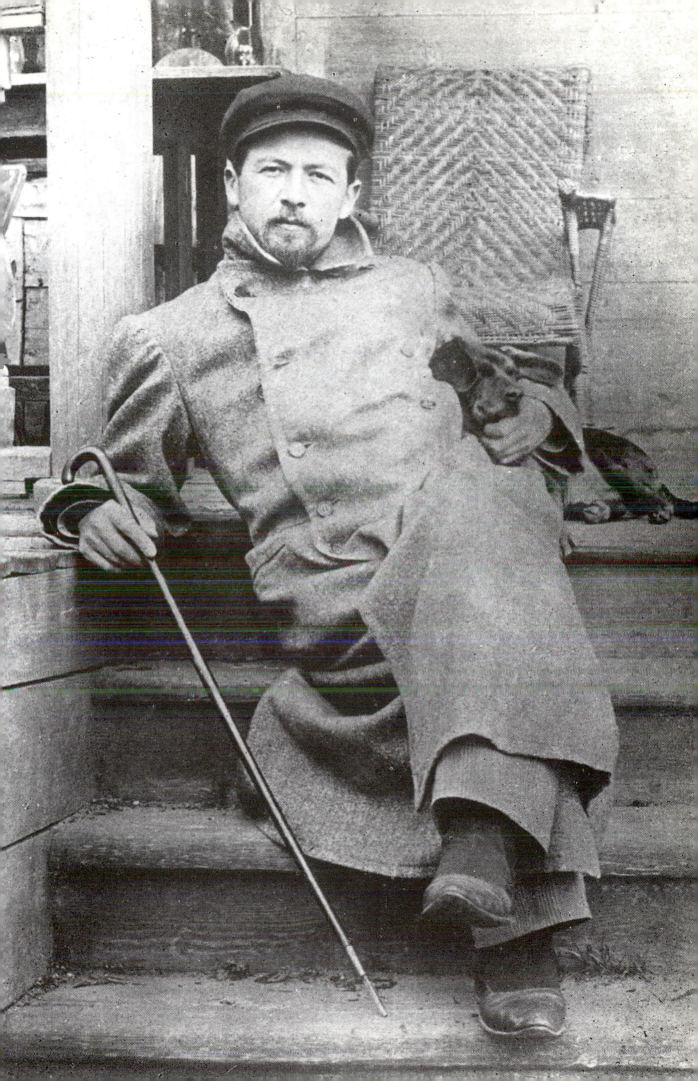

Scene from a 1989 production of The Cherry Orchard
Chekhov wrote his most popular play in 1904. The story of a bankrupt aristocratic Russian family that struggles in the face of major social and economic changes continues to captivate audiences today.

Surprised and encouraged by his popularity, Chekhov began to apply himself much more seriously to his work.

The following years saw the flowering of Chekhov's talent. His 700 to 800 short stories present a more complete picture of Russian society than can be found in the work of any of his contemporaries. Chekhov's humble origins meant that he had a much broader range of experience than most Russian writers. He could write confidently about people of all social classes.

The short story suited Chekhov, since he was more interested in character than in the twists and turns of plot. His stories often involve just a single event which sparks off a train of thought and feeling in his characters. In "The Kiss," published in 1887, for example, a soldier is kissed by a girl who mistakes him for someone else in the dark. This farcical event releases memories which make the soldier realize that his life is lonely and unhappy.

The tragedy of many of Chekhov's stories is that nothing happens. Either his characters do not have the courage to make changes in their lives, or, like the hero of "A Boring Story," published in 1889, they realize too late that they have made terrible mistakes. Chekhov himself was a cheerful man, but he believed that he had a responsibility as a writer to "soil his imagination with the grime of life." He told many difficult truths, and treated the unhappy characters in his stories with great sympathy.

Chekhov's kind nature can be seen in his life as well as in his work. In 1890, he made the long journey to Sakhalin, a prison colony, to study the notoriously

> "The writer must be humane to the tips of his fingers."
> (Anton Chekhov)

bad conditions there. In 1893, he published the results of his research in *The Island of Sakhalin*, a book that helped bring about changes in the colony. That year, in a short story, "Ward No. 6," he attacked the horrors of prison life, and criticized writers who ignored the suffering all around them, and preferred to spend their time in philosophical debate.

In 1897, Chekhov discovered that he had tuberculosis, a disease of the lungs. He spent most of his remaining years in Yalta, a Russian resort on the Black Sea, where the warm climate suited his fragile condition. A sociable man, Chekhov missed the activity of Moscow; he wrote that he felt like a transplanted tree, hesitating as to whether it should take root or wither.

A MASTER DRAMATIST

As well as fiction, Chekhov also wrote plays. His first great theatrical success was *The Seagull*, a play he had written in 1896. In 1898, the Moscow Art Theater performed it to huge acclaim. Chekhov followed this in 1901 with *The Three Sisters*, which tells of a family who dream of moving from their dreary home in the country, but never do. In his last play, *The Cherry Orchard*, Chekhov wrote about the decline of the Russian aristocracy. He felt that Russia's traditional rulers were losing their grip on the country—the Revolution of 1917 would prove him right. At the time, Chekhov's style—in which most of the action takes place offstage—was bold and unusual, but it would have a huge impact on 20th-century theater.

In 1901, Chekhov married Olga Knipper, an actress who had performed in *The Three Sisters*. Although they spent most of their marriage apart—he in Yalta for his health, and she in Moscow for her career—they wrote to each other almost daily. Olga accompanied her husband to a German health resort in June 1904, when his health took a turn for the worse. Chekhov died there on July 3, at the age of 44.

MAJOR WORKS	
1886	MOTLEY STORIES
1887	THE KISS
1889	A BORING STORY
1893	THE ISLAND OF SAKHALIN; WARD NO. 6
1896	THE SEAGULL
1901	THE THREE SISTERS
1904	THE CHERRY ORCHARD

EDITH WHARTON

Wealthy and well educated, Edith Wharton wrote about the often tragic conflict between individual happiness and the conventions of high society. Her novels charted the decline of the upper class in both America and Europe.

Edith Newbold Jones was born on January 24, 1862. Her parents, George and Lucretia, were very wealthy and distinguished members of the New York upper class. They owned spacious houses in both New York City and fashionable Newport, Rhode Island. To them, proper social manners and behavior were of great importance.

When the Civil War ended in 1865, property prices dropped sharply, reducing the family income. Thinking that life in Europe would be cheaper, Edith's adventurous father uprooted the family and sailed to France.

In Europe, George Jones played an important role in Edith's development: He taught her to read, encouraged her to become fluent in French, Italian, and German, and allowed her to use his library. His support had dramatic results: Edith began to write her first novel when she was just 11 years old. By 16, she had published a volume of poetry.

The Jones family returned to the United States around 1880. In late 1883, Edith met Edward Wharton, a wealthy banker. Twelve years her senior, "Teddy" was a kind gentleman with a warm, sociable nature. Edith was attracted by his easy sense of humor and his love of nature and animals. In April 1885, the couple married, and moved to Newport.

THE FIRST BOOK

Over the next few years, Wharton had poems and stories published in magazines. In 1897, her first book appeared. *The Great Decoration of Houses*—the result of her studies of architecture, furniture, and house design—was the first "how-to" decoration book ever published in America.

Wharton's knowledge of interior design would later make an appearance in her fiction. She often used the house as a symbol of women's lives. In a short

Edith Wharton, c.1885
Soon after Edith married Edward Wharton, the newlyweds traveled around Europe. This photograph was taken on the tour.

story of 1891, she wrote, "… a woman's nature is like a great house full of rooms." The sitting and drawing rooms were areas of social behavior, but "far beyond are other rooms, the handles of whose doors perhaps are never turned … and in the innermost room … the soul sits alone and waits for a footstep that never comes."

This passage may hint at the loneliness of her marriage: One of Wharton's associates likened Teddy to a "schoolboy in his tastes and in his mental development," a man who had no goals, and who was unmoved by art. He helped his wife to organize her financial affairs, but the more successful she became, the more he saw her talent as a kind of "witchcraft." Increasingly, he became impatient and self-absorbed.

Over the years, Teddy became more aggressive, and grew mentally unstable. Wharton herself often suffered from nervous illness—she had nearly died of typhoid as a child, and all her life suffered from recurring influenza, bronchitis, and asthma. Even so, she was a dedicated writer, working every morning. From 1899 to 1910, she published collections of short stories, several short novels, and two further books on house and garden decoration.

CRITICAL ACCLAIM

In 1905, she finally received the acclaim she had been hungering for with *The House of Mirth*, the first of her New York society novels. The heroine, Lily Bart, begins as an impressionable girl whose scheming mother urges her to use her beauty to gain wealth and social

NEW YORK HIGH SOCIETY

Wharton's novels depict the luxurious and exclusive world of Old New York's privileged upper class.

At the end of the 19th century, a group of wealthy families dominated New York society. Descendants of the Dutch and English settlers who had created large estates, these families owned property all over New York, and controlled the social and political life of the state. They had inherited huge fortunes, and many had no need to work at all. Their lives were a round of grand banquets, extravagant balls (*above right*), and other glittering events.

These self-styled aristocrats stood for sophistication and elegance—the "genteel tradition." They looked down on the newly rich, whom they thought vulgar.

position. Instead, Lily ends up penniless, and commits suicide. The book is a devastating satire on a corrupt upper class that values money over all else.

In 1907, the Whartons moved permanently to France. Teddy's mental state continued to deteriorate. Edith knew, however, that without the protection of marriage, women of her era could become lonely and poor. Even

Determined to protect their exclusive circle, the upper class produced the Social Register, a list of the 400 families who had not only wealth but "breeding"—correct manners and connections. To ensure this exclusivity, parents sometimes arranged marriages between their children and those of other families on the register, even if the couple barely knew each other.

Strict conventions governed behavior in this small, elite world. Often, this led to the kind of conflict between social expectations and personal ambitions that Wharton describes in her novels.

friendships with men of intellect—notably the writer Henry James.

In 1911, Wharton completed her next novel, *Ethan Frome*. Set on a New England farm, it is a tragic tale of thwarted love and wasted talents. The central character's love for a younger woman, and his creative aspirations, are frustrated by the stifling demands of social conventions.

Wharton returned to the subject of American high society with *The Age of Innocence*. The book, published in 1920, describes the frustrations of a New York lawyer, Newland Archer, who falls in love with Ellen Olenska, the separated wife of a Polish count. Archer is besotted with Ellen, but he does not pursue his feelings for fear of scandalizing society. In 1921, Wharton received the Pulitzer Prize for the book.

She won further honors in later life. In 1923, she became the first woman to receive an honorary degree from Yale University, and in the 1930s she was elected to both the National Institute of Arts and Letters and the American Academy of Arts and Letters. She died in France in 1937, at the age of 75.

when Teddy descended into manic depression, she put off committing him to an institution for as long as possible. It was only with reluctance that she finally divorced him in 1913.

Wharton never remarried. It seems that she knew that writing was her life's purpose. She admitted fearing "love's whole dark mystery," and its "devouring" quality. Instead, she cultivated

MAJOR WORKS

1899	THE GREATER INCLINATION
1905	THE HOUSE OF MIRTH
1911	ETHAN FROME
1920	THE AGE OF INNOCENCE
1934	A BACKWARD GLANCE

JACK LONDON

In his short life, Jack London produced more than 50 novels, as well as numerous short stories. With his tales of the Far North, he became one of the United States most popular novelists.

Jack London was born in San Francisco in 1876. His father was a traveling astrologer and his mother a spiritualist. Much of his boyhood was spent in poverty on the waterfront along San Francisco Bay. He had a poor education, and was often in trouble with the police. By the age of 16, he had already had several odd jobs, and had been on the road for a year as a tramp. On his return to San Francisco, he became an oyster pirate, robbing the oyster beds along the shore.

TRAVELS AND HARDSHIP

In his late teens, two experiences helped determine the course of London's life, and his future writing. At the age of 17, he ran away to sea to join a seal-hunting ship. The ship headed first to Japan, and then north to the Bering Sea, off the west coast of Alaska. This gave London his first taste of the icy wastes of the Far North.

When he returned home, the United States was experiencing severe economic problems. There was mass unemployment and London could not find work. In 1894, he joined thousands of fellow unemployed men on a march to Washington. The marchers were demanding that the nation create new jobs and support the poor. This early experience of unemployment and poverty made London a lifelong socialist. He believed that wealth should be distributed more equally. In many of the books he later wrote, he attacked the indifference of the rich toward the less well-off.

While working at odd jobs, London entered the University of California. He dropped out within the year, however—to work in a laundry—although he continued his studies on his own.

In 1896, he joined the gold rush to the Klondike region of Canada. He found no gold, but the experience inspired him to become a writer. In 1898,

Jack London
This undated photograph shows the writer early in his career.

he returned from Canada, and took a job as a construction worker. But that year, he had his first short story printed in a magazine, and he began to support himself through writing.

LITERARY SUCCESS

In 1900, London published his first book, *The Son of the Wolf*, a collection of short stories based on his time in the Klondike. Three years later, he produced a novel, *The Call of the Wild*. It told the story of a tamed wild dog, Buck, which after the death of its master answers the "call of the wild" and returns to his own kind to lead a pack of wolves. The book was a huge success, and made the writer's name.

Important literary magazines now regularly accepted his stories, which realistically described events rarely portrayed by other writers. Many of these were tales of courageous adventurers living close to nature. "To Build a Fire," for example, tells the story of a man's hopeless attempts to survive in the Arctic. London took some of his inspiration from the famous naturalist Charles Darwin's theories of evolution. Like Darwin, he believed that only the strongest could survive in a naturally cruel world.

Throughout the 1900s, London produced both fiction and nonfiction at an enormous rate. In 1903, he wrote *The People of the Abyss*, a study of the poor in the English capital, London. In this and another nonfiction work he wrote two years later, *The War of the Classes*, London expressed his controversial socialist theories.

WHITE FANG

The tale of a wild dog's hard life in the frozen north of America has become one of London's best-loved works.

London wrote *White Fang* after the phenomenal success he achieved with *The Call of the Wild*. Also set in the icy expanses of the Far North, it tells the story of a mongrel, three-quarters wolf and one-quarter dog, that is born wild but captured with his mother and raised by humans. White Fang becomes a fighting dog, and the novel tells of his struggles with other dogs. One of the book's most memorable chapters describes his battle with a bulldog named Cherokee, whose slow, relentless method of fighting contrasts with White Fang's savagery (*above right*).

In 1904, London published what some consider to be his best work, *The Sea-Wolf*. Based on his life at sea, the book tells of the struggle between Humphrey Van Weyden, an ordinary and unambitious seafarer, and Wolf Larsen, the ruthless captain of the *Ghost*. When the *Ghost* picks up Maude Brewster, a castaway, Van Weyden and Maude fall in love, making

The novel ends with White Fang making the reverse journey to that of Buck in *The Call of the Wild*. Whereas Buck obeyed its call and fled from civilization to return to the wilderness, White Fang becomes domesticated and lives on a California ranch, where he is renamed "The Blessed Wolf."

In 1909, London wrote *Martin Eden*. This semiautobiographical novel tells of a former sailor and laborer, who achieves literary success after a long struggle. Success brings its problems, however, and Eden comes to hate society. He goes on a long sea voyage and eventually kills himself.

LAST YEARS

London traveled widely as he became more successful, restless for new experiences that would bring him happiness. He went on many single-handed sea voyages, and visited the South Sea islands, Korea, Mexico, and Japan. He also pursued a parallel career as a journalist, covering the war between Russia and Japan (1904-05) for a newspaper. He later recorded these experiences in his fiction, notably in *South Sea Tales*, published in 1911.

London earned over a million dollars from his writing, but he was still unhappy. He became dependent on alcohol as a way to escape the misery he observed in the world. On November 22, 1916, London committed suicide by taking an overdose of sleeping pills.

Larsen intensely jealous. Eventually, the couple manage to escape from the deranged captain, who runs the ship aground on a deserted island and dies.

Two of London's other significant novels soon followed. In 1908, *The Iron Heel*, a vision of a socialist future, was published. It was immediately banned in many parts of the United States because of its radical ideas.

MAJOR WORKS

1903	THE CALL OF THE WILD
1904	THE SEA-WOLF
1906	WHITE FANG
1908	THE IRON HEEL
1909	MARTIN EDEN
1911	SOUTH SEA TALES

GIUSEPPE VERDI

Born into a humble Italian family, Giuseppe Verdi became one of the greatest opera composers of all time. His music, still regularly performed today, inspired Italians as they fought to unify their country in the 1860s.

Giuseppe Verdi was born in 1813 in Le Roncole, a village in the duchy of Parma, northern Italy. His parents ran the local tavern and grocery store. They recognized their son's musical talents, and before he was eight, his father had bought him a spinet, a keyboard instrument like a piano.

A MUSICAL EDUCATION

Verdi progressed so well that he soon became the village organist. But Le Roncole could not offer the education he required. So, one of his father's associates, Antonio Barezzi, paid for Verdi to go to school in Busseto, a nearby town. He also paid for the boy to have extra lessons from Ferdinando Provesi, head of Busseto's music school and organist in the town's cathedral.

By the age of 16, Verdi had become famous in Busseto, sometimes playing in the cathedral instead of Provesi. But in late 1831, he decided to go to Milan, where he hoped to enroll at the Conservatory, one of the best music schools

in Italy. The Conservatory refused him entry, however, saying he was too old and not talented enough. Instead, he took lessons from a pianist at La Scala, Milan's celebrated opera house.

In 1835, Verdi returned to Busseto, and became a teacher at his old music school. The job gave him a secure salary, allowing him to marry Margherita Barezzi, Antonio's daughter. During his time at Busseto, Verdi wrote a number of marches and some church music, but his heart was not in this work. He wanted to produce operas. In early 1839, he moved back to Milan, determined to achieve his ambitious goals.

His determination soon paid off. That year, his first opera, *Oberto*, was successfully produced at La Scala. The opera house's manager, Bartolomeo Merelli, offered Verdi a contract to write more operas. Then tragedy

Giuseppe Verdi, 1881, by Giovanni Boldini
This elegant picture, by the fashionable Italian portrait painter Boldini, shows the composer at the age of 68.

struck. Verdi's baby son died, followed by his wife the following year, 1840. To add to his troubles, his second opera was withdrawn after just one performance, when the audience hissed and booed. Utterly depressed, Verdi vowed never to write another opera. But with Merelli's encouragement, Verdi recovered his nerve and wrote *Nabucco*, based on the biblical story of King Nebuchadnezzar. First performed in 1842, *Nabucco* established Verdi's reputation in Italy and beyond.

FAME AND FRICTION

In the 1840s, Verdi produced at least one opera a year, including *Macbeth*, based on William Shakespeare's play, which is now considered to be Verdi's first masterpiece. But his prolific output came with a price: He suffered increasingly from stress-related illnesses.

By the late 1840s, Verdi was internationally famous and his works were in demand throughout Europe. On a trip to Paris in 1847, he met an old friend of his, Giuseppina Strepponi, a singing teacher. They fell in love, and by 1849 they were living together. Verdi was very happy with this warm and intelligent woman, and in the next ten years he produced three of his greatest works: *Rigoletto*, *Il Trovatore*, and *La Traviata*. The couple married in 1859, spending most of their time in Busseto.

A NATIONALIST FIGURE

By now, Verdi had emerged as a musical spokesperson for the movement fighting for the unification of Italy. The composer had lived most of his life in

OPERA'S GOLDEN AGE

The spirit of Romanticism inspired Italian composers to write some of the most passionate operas of all time.

As Romanticism swept across Europe in the early 19th century, it sparked off a radically new style of opera in Italy. Italian Romantic composers left behind the stiff and rigid traditions of 18th-century opera, and turned to writing dramas full of passion. Displays of intense, unrestrained emotions from the characters gave rise to virtuoso singing performances, and the star singer became the rage.

Composers such as Gioacchino Rossini and Gaetano Donizetti filled their works with passages designed to show off the powers of their celebrity singers. Some of their "mad scenes," where the

a divided Italy. His home state of Parma was under French control when he was born, and Milan was part of the Austrian empire. The rest of Italy consisted of several semi-independent kingdoms. Verdi, like many Italians, hoped that one day the country would be united. He often expressed this intense nationalism in his operas, which provided vital inspiration to his fellow countrymen.

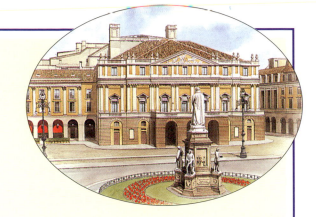

singer seemed to be crazy, demanded precise and highly skilled vocal acrobatics.

But some composers felt that these singers overpowered the music. Verdi himself preferred a more realistic style of singing. By the early 1850s, when he wrote *Rigoletto*, *La Traviata*, and *Il Trovatore*, he had begun to get rid of the virtuoso displays typical of earlier composers. Instead, he used the orchestra more imaginatively, expressing characters and dramatic situations with music rather than with voices. Verdi's advances culminated with his masterpiece *Otello*, which premiered at Milan's La Scalà opera house (*above*) in 1887.

In 1861, after a number of armed uprisings, nationalists declared a new kingdom of Italy. By 1870, the whole country was united, with Rome as its capital. When the first parliament of the new kingdom was established in 1861, Verdi was representative for Busseto, although he resigned four years later.

In 1871, Verdi completed a new opera to celebrate the opening of the Suez Canal in Egypt. *Aïda*, set in ancient Egypt, was a great success at its premiere in the Egyptian capital, Cairo.

Verdi's creativity continued into old age. In his 74th year, he produced *Otello*, and six years later, a comic masterpiece, *Falstaff*. He was now also involved in charitable projects, including the Casa di Riposo, a rest home in Milan for retired musicians. But the old man had not completely mellowed: When the Milan Conservatory requested that it be renamed in his honor, he refused, observing sharply, "They wouldn't have me young, so they shan't have me old."

In 1897, Giuseppina died. Verdi was devastated. Four years later, while staying in Milan, he had a brain hemorrhage. On January 27, 1901, after a few days in a coma, he died. He was 87. In a magnificent ceremony, he was buried alongside his wife in the Casa di Riposo. Two hundred thousand people lined Milan's black-draped streets to pay their respects to a man whose music had inspired the world, and complemented the history of modern Italy.

MAJOR WORKS	
1842	NABUCCO
1847	MACBETH
1851	RIGOLETTO
1853	IL TROVATORE; LA TRAVIATA
1871	AÏDA
1887	OTELLO
1893	FALSTAFF

RICHARD WAGNER

With his arrogant and selfish nature, and controversial views on art, life, and politics, Wagner made many bitter enemies during his career. Yet his "music dramas" changed the course of opera music forever.

Richard Wagner was born on May 22, 1813, in Leipzig, a city in eastern Germany. It is not certain who his father was. His legal father, Friedrich Wagner, died when Richard was only six months old. The next year, Richard's mother, Johanna, married Ludwig Geyer, who may have been Wagner's real father.

LATE DEVELOPER

Wagner is unusual among composers in showing no musical skill until he was in his twenties. He never even learned to play an instrument. Even so, in 1831, he enrolled at Leipzig University as a music student. At first, he was carried away by student life. He drank heavily, gambled, and even challenged fellow students to sword fights. But eventually, he devoted himself to his studies.

In 1833, Wagner started his first job, as rehearsal conductor at the theater in Würzburg, central Germany. It was here that he first became interested in opera production, and he wrote his first complete opera, *The Fairies*.

From Würzburg, Wagner moved farther north to Magdeburg to become conductor of the city's opera company. In Magdeburg, he met Minna Planer, an actress, whom he married in 1836.

Wagner was very bad with money, and spent most of his life avoiding creditors. As the debts piled up, Minna lost patience. When Wagner was summoned to meet his creditors, Minna ran off with a businessman. But then Wagner fled to Riga, in Russia, and she rejoined him. After less than two years, during which he began work on an opera, *Rienzi*, Wagner's creditors caught up with him again. His passport was confiscated, and he and Minna had to be smuggled across the Russian frontier to Prussia, and from there to England. They then sailed on to Paris.

Wagner was soon in desperate financial straits again, and was imprisoned

Richard Wagner, 1871,
by Franz von Lenbach
This shows Wagner at the age of 58, around the time he was completing the *Ring* cycle.

briefly for his debts. While in jail, he finished *Rienzi*, which had its premiere in Dresden in 1842. The performance began at six in the evening. When it finally ended, at midnight, the audience responded with rapturous applause.

This success was followed by another when *The Flying Dutchman* was first performed in 1843. After this, Wagner was appointed concertmaster of the Dresden Opera. *Tannhäuser* followed two years later.

While in Dresden, Wagner began work on *The Ring of the Nibelung*, a cycle of four operas based on ancient Scandinavian legend. Several times, he laid aside this huge project, fearing it would never be performed.

EXILE AND RETURN

In 1849, Wagner took part in an uprising in Dresden. When the revolt failed, he and Minna fled to Zurich, Switzerland. For the next 15 years, while his operas were gaining enthusiastic audiences all over Europe, Wagner remained in exile from his native country. In Zurich, Otto Wesendonck, a wealthy merchant, became a champion of his music, providing the Wagners with a villa close to his own. In return, Richard fell in love with Otto's wife, Mathilde. Spurred by his passion, Wagner began to compose *Tristan and Isolde*. He also continued to work on the *Ring* cycle.

Wagner's relationship with Mathilde broke up when Minna discovered one of the couple's love letters. In 1859, the Wagners moved to Paris. Three years later, their marriage was over. Wagner went to Vienna, the Austrian capital, but

---

WAGNER'S THEORIES

All his life, Wagner wrote passionate and controversial essays on a wide range of subjects.

Wagner wrote almost as many essays as musical works. He covered such varied subjects as vegetarianism, the treatment of animals, feminism, and the place of Jews in society. But most of his writing was on art and music.

At first, Wagner wrote in the most popular opera style of the day, valuing the singing and dancing more highly than the music. But in 1849, he wrote an essay, *Art and Revolution*, outlining the concept of the "music drama." His theory was to treat poetry, dance, and music as equals in a "total art-work." To do this, he added new, more expressive instruments to the orchestra and

---

had to flee the city in 1864, after running up large debts. By this time, it was safe for him to return to Germany, and he settled in Munich, in Bavaria. There, in 1865, *Tristan and Isolde* premiered, with Hans von Bülow conducting. Von Bülow's wife, Cosima—the daughter of the famous Hungarian composer Franz Liszt—captivated Wagner. They soon started an affair.

created rich harmonies that expressed powerful emotions. With the *Ring* cycle (*above*), he also mastered the use of *leitmotivs*—recurring themes that represent persons, events, or ideas.

For Wagner, the reform of opera went hand-in-hand with social reform. He saw the opera festival as a way of uniting "the folk." One of the reasons he built the Bayreuth Festival Theater was to house his social ideals.

In Munich, the composer became friends with King Ludwig of Bavaria. The king cleared Wagner's debts and paid him a yearly pension to complete the *Ring* cycle. Together, they planned to build a theater designed specifically for Wagner's operas. Meanwhile, Cosima was pregnant with Wagner's child, and she left her husband. The couple moved to Lucerne, Switzerland. In 1869, the von Bülows finally divorced, and Cosima was free to marry Wagner.

In the early 1870s, as he completed the *Ring* cycle, Wagner was still looking for somewhere to build his theater. Eventually, he chose Bayreuth, in Bavaria. In 1872, he moved to the town, and began raising funds for the project. The town council donated the site, and King Ludwig agreed to pay for the enterprise. The theater opened on August 13, 1876, with a performance of the entire *Ring* cycle—*The Rhine Gold, The Valkyries, Siegfried,* and *The Twilight of the Gods*—over four nights. This has continued ever since as the annual Bayreuth Festival.

By now, Wagner was having heart attacks. His last opera, *Parsifal*, had its premiere at Bayreuth in July 1882. It had 15 more performances, the last of which Wagner conducted. After the performance, Cosima and Wagner left for Venice, where he intended to carry on working. But he had a final heart attack on February 13, 1883, and died in Cosima's arms. He was buried with great ceremony at Bayreuth.

MAJOR WORKS

1842	RIENZI
1843	THE FLYING DUTCHMAN
1845	TANNHÄUSER
1850	LOHENGRIN
c.1848-74	THE RING OF NIBELUNG
1865	TRISTAN AND ISOLDE

JOHN PHILIP SOUSA

Sousa's marches made him a millionaire before the turn of the century, and America's most popular bandleader ever. His stirring military music encouraged patriotism in the United States during a turbulent period.

John Philip Sousa was born in Washington, D.C., on November 6, 1854. His father, Antonio, had been born in Spain to Portuguese parents, and his mother was Bavarian. Antonio was a trombonist with the U.S. Marine Band.

A PASSION FOR MUSIC

John was educated at local schools until he was 13. He also went to a music school, where he studied violin and orchestration, as well as trombone, alto horn, and cornet. When he was 13, the boy loved music so much he wanted to run away with a circus band. Instead, his father enrolled him as an apprentice in the U.S. Marine Band.

Sousa served in the band for nearly seven years. He was now beginning to compose. He wrote his first piece in 1872, a dance for piano called *Moonlight on the Potomac Waltzes*. He also produced his first march, *The Review*, the same year.

Sousa left the Marine Band in 1875, and played in a variety of local ensembles. The next year, he moved to Philadelphia, where he joined the violin section of an orchestra. He also began working as a conductor.

In 1879, Sousa conducted and toured with a production of an operetta—a light musical drama—*HMS Pinafore*. The tour was a success. Sousa married a member of the cast, Jane van Middlesworth Bellis. The same year, a telegram summoned him to return to the U.S. Marine Band—this time as its director. He was still only 25 years old.

Sousa had no experience in conducting a military band, but plenty of ambition. He developed the Marine Band, and brought in more musicians. He was now working on his first operetta, *The Smugglers*. By 1885, he had had three operettas produced, and was working on two more.

Meanwhile, Sousa was earning a wider reputation for his marches. His

John Philip Sousa
In this undated picture, the band leader proudly displays his service medals.

The Marine Band at the White House
This picture shows Sousa leading the band while guests file past on their way to a dinner hosted by President and Mrs. Theodore Roosevelt, early in the 20th century.

earliest successes came in 1886, with *The Gladiator* and *The Rifle Regiment*. In 1888, he wrote one of his most famous marches, *Semper Fidelis*, and the following year, *The Washington Post*. The *Post* achieved international fame; the march was closely associated with a new dance, the two-step. By now, Sousa was an international celebrity. Soon he would earn his enduring nickname, the "March King."

The U.S. Marine Band toured across the United States in 1891 and 1892. Sousa then resigned from the Marine Band and set up his own group. The Sousa Band played its first concert in New Jersey in September 1892. The band would go on to become the most popular of its kind in American history.

Sousa was a sound businessman. In 1892, he negotiated royalty deals for his compositions—meaning he would receive payment for each copy of the sheet music bought or performed. This secured his financial future.

During the 1890s, Sousa had also designed his own bass tuba, with a large mushroom-shaped bell pointing up into the air, and a looping body designed to encircle the player from the left shoulder down to his right side. The manufacturer named it the sousaphone.

Success piled upon success for Sousa. In 1895, the first major production of one of his operettas, *El Capitan*, took place. The work was very successful. But Sousa's fame reached its peak in 1897 with the publication of his brisk march, *The Stars and Stripes Forever!* This stirring and patriotic work was everyone's favorite.

THE SOUSA BAND

Sousa's band played concerts at expositions, fairs, and concert halls. Life was a hectic cycle of up to four performances a day, seven days a week. Sousa paid some of America's best musicians to perform with him, and by the turn of the century, his band could name its price for public appearances.

The band was also successful overseas. During the first decade of the century, it made four tours of Europe, and in 1910, embarked on a year-long world tour. One estimate says that in the course of its career, Sousa's band traveled more than a million miles.

The life of the band did not stop Sousa from experimenting. He was eager to include other instruments—the band grew to some 70 members in the 1920s—and tried introducing voices. By now, Sousa's success had made him wealthy. But he still continued to tour and to compose at a great rate. He wrote many marches and operettas, as well as songs and other vocal music.

Despite Sousa's other activities, the center of his career remained touring with his band. In 1914, however, the outbreak of World War I brought the tours to a halt. Sousa signed up for the U.S. Navy, where he trained military bands; he also toured with a 300-strong naval band. To help the war effort, Sousa took only a dollar a week in pay.

After the war's end in 1918, Sousa returned to touring with his band. By now he was in his sixties, and his health was beginning to fail. Yet he continued to tour even after 1929, when the Depression began to affect the entertainment industry. Finally, in 1931, Sousa broke up the band.

Sousa continued to compose and conduct other bands and ensembles until his death. He died of a heart attack on March 6, 1932, after rehearsing a band in Reading, Pennsylvania. One report claims that the last piece of music he ever conducted was *The Stars and Stripes Forever!*

A critic later summed up Sousa's enduring popularity: "His marches are still played and they will continue to be played wherever a public occasion calls for communal rejoicing or even mass hysteria."

MAJOR WORKS

1872	MOONLIGHT ON THE POTOMAC WALTZES; THE REVIEW
1888	SEMPER FIDELIS
1889	THE WASHINGTON POST
1895	EL CAPITAN
1897	THE STARS AND STRIPES FOREVER!

SCOTT JOPLIN

Many details of Scott Joplin's life are unknown, and he was forgotten until the 1960s, when his music enjoyed a revival. He is now recognized as the "King of Ragtime," and a great and original composer.

Scott Joplin was born around November 24, 1868, probably in Marshall, Texas, or Shreveport, Louisiana. His father, Giles, was a former slave. His duties had included playing the violin in his master's home. Joplin's mother, Florence, worked as caretaker of the church in Texarkana, Arkansas. Scott had three brothers and two sisters.

AN EARLY TALENT

Joplin grew up in Texarkana. His talent for music was obvious from an early age. Giles Joplin deserted the family, and Florence had to do housework for neighbors to help support herself and the children. She took Scott with her, and he was allowed to play the piano in some of the houses. Eventually, his mother bought an old piano so he could play at home. By the time he was a teenager, he was playing in local churches and for social events. He could also play the guitar, mandolin, and cornet.

Joplin's musical outlook was influenced by two sources: the local African American churches, where he enjoyed the lively gospel music, and the clubs and bars—known as "honky-tonks"—where he came across march tunes.

PLAYING AND WRITING

When he was 16 or 17, Joplin left home to become a traveling musician. He played the piano and sang in a group named the Texas Medley Quartette that included one of his brothers. The group seems to have traveled widely.

In 1893, Joplin went to the World's Fair in Chicago. At the fair, he organized a brass band and met several musicians who encouraged him to write down his own compositions. Two years later, Joplin's first publications—two waltz songs, "Please Say You Will" and "A Picture of Her Face"—were issued in New York.

By this time, Joplin had settled in Sedalia, Missouri. Ever determined to

Scott Joplin
This undated drawing of the composer captures his sensitive nature.

widen his knowledge, he took music courses at the newly opened George R. Smith College for African Americans. He also gave music lessons and performed at various places in Sedalia, including the Maple Leaf Club, a social center for African Americans.

MAPLE LEAF RAG

In the summer of 1899, John Stark, the owner of a music publishing company in Sedalia, heard Joplin play one of his pieces. He immediately offered to publish it. The piece was called "Maple Leaf Rag."

"Maple Leaf Rag" was not the first piece of ragtime music to be published. Other composers had written ragtime music, and Joplin himself had published "Original Rags" earlier in 1899. None of these pieces, however, enjoyed the success, of "Maple Leaf Rag." Joplin had told a pupil, "'Maple Leaf Rag' will make me king of ragtime composers"—and it did. Within a few years, hundreds of thousands of copies were sold. It started a new era in American music.

THE RAGTIME CRAZE

Over the next few years, America went crazy over ragtime. Some people scoffed at it—but young people could not get enough of the lively music that could be heard on every street where there was a bar. Even European classical composers, such as Claude Debussy, were entranced by ragtime, and made use of it in some of their compositions.

Joplin always thought of himself as a serious composer, and considered his ragtime music worthy of being ranked

JOPLIN AND RAGTIME

At the end of the 19th century, a new kind of music swept America— ragtime.

Joplin was the king of ragtime, a style of music in which a syncopated melody is played over a steady, marchlike accompaniment. Syncopation is the practice in music of creating accents where they are not expected. This is the essence of ragtime: It is the syncopated effect that gives the music its catchy, toe-tapping quality.

Meanwhile, the pianist's left hand keeps the rhythm, or pulse. In ragtime, this is usually duple meter—a steady ONE two, ONE two. This combination of melody and march can be heard in Joplin's best-known rag, "The Entertainer" (*above right*).

alongside the finest classics. He composed some 40 piano rags in all, plus another seven with collaborators. Their richness of harmony distinguishes them from most other ragtime music.

During 1899, Joplin began creating a large-scale work of several dances in rag style. This was the first rag ballet, *The Ragtime Dance*. Later, he wrote the words and music of an opera, *A Guest*

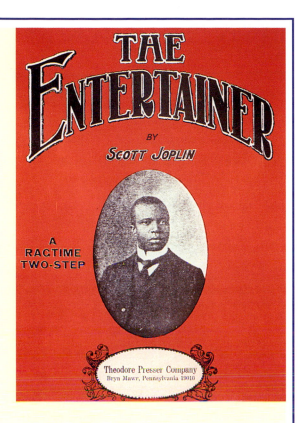

Ragtime originated in African American communities in St. Louis and other centers along the Mississippi River in the late 1800s. The music evolved from slave plantation songs and a dance named the "cakewalk." Initially written for piano, ragtime music was also influenced by black spirituals and gospel music.

of Honor (1903). Neither work was successful, and neither survives today.

Joplin wrote a manual of rag music, *The School of Ragtime*, which was published in 1908. The commentary reveals how seriously Joplin regarded his art. He wrote: "That real ragtime of the higher class is rather difficult to play is a painful truth which most pianists have discovered …." Joplin felt that many pianists lost the effect of ragtime by playing it too fast: the tempo should be similar to that of a moderate march.

PERSONAL LIFE

Details of Joplin's personal life are sketchy. Around 1900, he married Belle Hayden, the sister-in-law of one of his piano students. The couple lived in St. Louis for several years before their marriage ended. When he moved to New York in 1907, Joplin met Lottie Stokes, whom he married two years later.

Joplin's friendship with his publisher John Stark ended in 1909, when Stark refused to publish *A Guest of Honor*. Stark also ignored *Treemonisha*, Joplin's second opera. Finally, Joplin published it himself in 1911. He scraped together the money himself to mount just a single, inadequate performance in 1915. He had to do without scenery, costumes, or orchestra. Not surprisingly, the opera attracted almost no attention from either critics or the public.

Its failure devastated Joplin. Already suffering mental difficulties, he was hospitalized in New York in 1916. Joplin died on April 1, 1917, at the age of 49.

MAJOR WORKS

1895	PLEASE SAY YOU WILL; A PICTURE OF HER FACE
1899	ORIGINAL RAGS; MAPLE LEAF RAG
1902	THE ENTERTAINER
1903	A GUEST OF HONOR
1911	TREEMONISHA

GLOSSARY

abstract art Art that does not represent objects or people that can be recognized in the real world, but that expresses a thought, idea, or feeling through colors and shapes.

apprentice A person who learns a trade or craft by working and studying with an experienced master.

canvas A firm, closely woven cloth on which an artist paints a picture.

classical music A term meaning the opposite of light, popular, or folk music. Classical music emphasizes order and clarity, and aims for formal beauty rather than emotional expression. It is usually considered to have permanent rather than short-lived value.

commission An order received by an artist, writer, or composer from a patron to produce a work of art, literature, or music.

composition The arrangement or organization of the various elements of a work of art, literature, or music.

ensemble From the French word meaning "together," the term refers to any combination of performers, but especially a small group of musicians.

fiction A type of literature, such as novels and short stories, in which the characters and events are invented.

genre painting Paintings depicting ordinary scenes from daily life.

landscape A kind of painting showing a view of natural scenery, such as mountains or forests.

march A piece of music composed to accompany the orderly progress of a large group of people, usually soldiers. It is one of the earliest forms of music.

medium Term used to describe the various methods and materials of the artist, such as oil paint on canvas.

music drama A term first used by Richard Wagner to describe operas in which the music, songs, and story are all of equal value.

novel An invented story that is usually long and complex, and deals especially with human experience.

oil paint A technique developed in the 15th century in which colors, or pigments, are mixed with the slow-drying and flexible medium of oil.

opera A dramatic musical work, first developed in late-16th-century

Italy, in which the characters sing the text, accompanied by an orchestra.

operetta Italian for "little opera," the term refers to a light play with music, songs, and dances.

patron A person or organization that asks an artist, writer, or composer to create a work of art, literature, or music. Usually the patron pays for the work.

portrait A drawing, painting, photograph, or sculpture that gives a likeness of a person and often provides an insight into his or her personality.

print A picture produced by pressing a piece of paper against a variety of inked surfaces, including engraved metal plates and wooden blocks. There are several different methods of making prints, including engraving and etching.

prose One of the two major forms of literature, the other being poetry. With its greater irregularity and variety of rhythm, prose is closer to everyday language than poetry.

ragtime An early type of jazz music popular from around 1890 to 1920. It is particularly associated with piano playing in which the left hand provides harmony and rhythm, while the right hand plays the melody.

Romanticism An early 19th-century European movement in art, literature, and music that was a reaction to the restraint and order of the 18th-century style. The Romantics emphasized the free expression of emotion and imagination, passion, love of nature and exotic places, individual liberty, and social reform. They rejected all strict rules governing the creation of art, and opposed technological progress. In the United States, Thomas Cole and the Hudson River School of artists used a Romantic style to paint the native American landscape.

sketch A rough or quick version of a picture, often produced as a trial run for a more finished work.

still life A drawing or painting of objects that cannot move by themselves, such as fruit or flowers.

style The distinctive appearance of a particular artist, writer, or composer's work of art.

symbol An object which represents something else; for example, a dove commonly symbolizes peace.

Symbolism A movement developed in France in the late 19th century. The Symbolists expressed ideas, emotions, and moods through color and line.

syncopation A musical device in which stress is placed on notes where it is not expected. This produces an unusual, irregular rhythm.

technique The way an artist uses his or her materials.

FURTHER READING

Englander, Robert. *Opera! What's All the Screaming About?* Walker, 1983

Ingpen, Robert R., illus. *The Industrial Revolution.* Text by Michael Pollard and Philip Wilkinson. Chelsea House, 1995

Janson, H.W. *The History of Art.* Abrams, 1995 (standard reference)

Lyttle, Richard B. *Mark Twain—The Man and His Adventure.* Simon & Schuster Children's, 1994

The New Grove Dictionary of Music and Musicians. Grove's Dictionaries of Music, 1980 (standard reference)

Otfinoski, Stephen. *Nineteenth Century Writers.* Facts on File, 1991

Powell, Jillian. *Art in the Nineteenth Century: Art and Artists.* Thomson Learning, 1994

Preston, Kitty. *Scott Joplin.* Chelsea House, 1988

Reyero, Carlos. *The Key to Art from Romanticism to Impressionism.* Lerner Group, 1990

Tames, Richard. *Giuseppe Verdi.* Franklin Watts, 1991

INDEX

Picture Credits